Christmas Confessions & Cocktails

A HUMOROUS HOLIDAY MEMOIR
with SASSY DRINK RECIPES

VICKI LESAGE

press

Published by Party Girl Press
Copyright © 2015 by Vicki Lesage

ISBN-13: 978-1515037576
ISBN-10: 1515037576

Cover design by Ellen Meyer and Clara Vidal
Author photo by Mickaël Lesage and Damien Croisot

CATCH UP ON THE
Confessions Series
BY BESTSELLING AUTHOR VICKI LESAGE

For deals, news releases, and a free ecopy of
Confessions & Cocktails, sign up here:
http://bit.ly/lesage-news

*To Grandpa and Grandma, who appear
in some of these stories but have inspired
every single one*

Table of Contents

Introduction

Bonjour mes amis!

We might not be friends yet but I hope by the end of this holiday-themed book, you'll feel like we've sat down and had a few laughs over more than a few drinks.

My previous memoirs, *Confessions of a Paris Party Girl*, *Confessions of a Paris Potty Trainer*, and *Petite Confessions*, were written in semi-chronological order, offering embarrassing glimpses into my life in Paris and background on how I ended up here.

This memoir is a little different. I decided to take two things I love—Christmas and cocktails—throw them in a martini shaker, and mix up a fun, seasonal collection for you. Each essay has a tenuous tie to Christmas, whether humorous or heartwarming. If you've read my previous books (*merci*, you're the best!), you might recognize a few of the stories, ones that were too important to be left out of this book. But most of these stories are brand spankin' new.

Oh, and each one is paired with a cocktail that ties in

to the story's theme.

So drink up (responsibly, of course) and enjoy this holiday collection!

Vicki Lesage
Paris, 2015

It's The Thought That Counts

Atrocious presents and off-the-wall gift-giving traditions

1

Sold, to the Woman in the Reindeer Sweater

"It's the thought that counts" doesn't even come close to applying when you exchange gifts with 50+ people. You'd be lucky to remember to even purchase a gift for each person, much less have time to put any thought into it.

My mom is one of nine children, and between her and my aunts and uncles, they have 39 kids. Then we all started having kids. But Grandma and Grandpa's house had been a zoo long before then.

We could never get an exact headcount (people have this annoying habit of wanting to grab another beer or actually enjoy themselves instead of staying put while you count them), but it usually hit upwards of 55 people. Even with a modest 40-odd guests, chaos ensued.

The adults used to do a Secret Santa, where Grandma took gift ideas from everyone and called up everyone else to tell them what to buy. She was essentially an unpaid central clearinghouse for the exchange of money in the form of gifts that would still likely be returned.

She put an end to that, citing that her time was better spent playing bingo at church. No one protested because my family loves bingo. But what would we do instead?

First, we tried Rob Your Neighbor. Everyone picked a gently used object from their house and wrapped it up. Then we drew numbers to see who got to pick first from the steaming pile of crap under the tree. The subsequent person could either steal your crappy gift or pick a new gift they hoped would be less crappy.

They never were. My family clearly played fast and loose with the definition of "gently used." Beer steins with broken wooden handles, embroidered throw pillows with sayings like "If you want breakfast in bed, best sleep in the kitchen", and soap dispensers adorned with a skunk were among the pickings.

We decided to up the ante. You had to buy a shiny new gift. Minimum price: $10.

That helped, but people tended to buy stuff they wanted for themselves, or stuff that was just weird. Christmas of '07 was The War of the Travel Wrench Set. I couldn't imagine one person wanting a miniature wrench set that badly, much less half my family. But that thing got robbed so many times we had to institute a new rule that the same gift could only be stolen three times. Then the rest of the game was full of floral-scented candles and Christmas tea towels that didn't even get stolen once.

We increased the limit to $20. That meant there was more expensive crap under the tree, but it was mostly still crap. With a family that big, you can't possibly choose a gift that will appeal to everyone. Men and women, boys and girls, ages 10 to 80+... it's inconceivable!

In Christmas of '09 my cousin's girlfriend brought a

penguin-shaped martini shaker with a variety pack of drink mixes. I HAD TO HAVE IT. My uncle had the first turn and picked it, but didn't seem too interested in it. He was probably hoping for a travel wrench set. My turn was next, so I promptly stole it. It's mine, all mine! I don't think I said that out loud, but I might have. I *really* wanted that martini shaker.

I was thrilled to have scored such a great gift so early on, but then realization dawned. Anyone else in the room could steal it. GAH!!! What if I got stuck with a tea towel or a candle? I *needed* this martini shaker. I broke out into a cold sweat every time someone took their turn. *Please don't steal it, please don't steal it.* My cousins sensed my malaise and would jokingly reach for my gift on their turns, only to go instead for a deep fryer or a huge jar of peanut M&M's. There you go, move along. Leave me in peace with my $20 martini shaker that I could have just bought myself and saved a lot of stress and armpit stains.

Finally, after a torturous number of turns, the game was over. The martini shaker had successfully remained in my sweaty possession.

Noting my wracked nerves, my mom proposed a solution. Ever the bookworm, her idea was to conduct a book auction.

"We all bring any books we're done with—only good condition here, folks—and we'll auction them off," she shouted above the din.

"What?" fifty-five family members replied.

"We can have a fun little auction, score some new books, and give the money to charity!"

"What?" we all shouted.

"I think she said something about charity?'

"No, it was about books!"

"It was about both!" I shouted. Where was my karaoke microphone when I needed it? Answer: Far, far away from my martini shaker, for the good of all those around me.

Somehow we managed to make ourselves heard, and the plan was set for the auction the following year. Christmas rolled around and everyone brought their gently used books. And Mom brought her karaoke microphone (like mother, like daughter).

"Testing, 1, 2, 3, testing," Mom said. She was really getting a kick out of this. "First up, let's discuss the charity. Vicki has selected Heifer International, which provides animals to impoverished villages around the world. Depending on how much money we raise tonight, we could send a goat, a sheep, or even a cow!"

"Oooh, we could send honeybees to Guatemala," one of my cousins said, flipping through the catalogue.

"Or a llama to Bolivia," another cousin suggested. "It says here they can make fabric from the wool and then sell the fabric to neighboring villages."

That sounded good. The whole teach-a-man-to-fish thing.

"Look, here's a school of fish," my uncle chimed in.

Or give actual fish.

"I want to send a water buffalo to Nepal," my brother, Stephen, said. Of course he would pick the biggest animal on the list.

"Well, that's the most expensive one," I said in my big sister voice, even though we were both grown and he towered over me, "so we'd better earn a lot at this auction!"

"OK, everyone," Mom said. "Let the bidding begin!'

Everyone cheered. We are a seriously dorky family.

"We'll start with a steamy romance," Mom said. "One dollar."

"One dollar," Grandma bid, raising her index finger.

"Grandma, that's your book!" I said. "That's from the stack you donated!"

"Oh, then that's why it looks so good! I bid one

dollar on the next romance."

"OK," Mom said, "but let's finish with this one first. One steamy romance, with Fabio on the cover. Do I hear one dollar?"

We managed to unload some of Grandma's Stash O' Trash, but as she was the most avid romance reader in the bunch, she'd donated way more than the rest of the group could take on. When the few other romance books came up for auction, she snapped them right up for a pretty penny. Which is easy when you don't have competition, but wasn't contributing much money to the pot.

Not to mention, attention was waning as most people weren't interested in Fabio's latest tryst. "I'll buy all the remaining romances for $30," Grandma offered.

"Sold! To the lady in the reindeer sweater," Mom said.

The auction continued as we went through the genres.

"Here's a sci-fi thriller about alien robots living in the center of the earth. It's really good. Let's go ahead and pair it with this sci-fi thriller about cyborgs."

For every person who made a face about alien robots and cyborgs, there'd be another person waving dollar bills around, eager to find out what happened to the alien robots and cyborgs. The group's tastes were just eclectic enough that every book sold, even if only for a dollar.

"Next up, *A Man, A Can, A Plan*. It says here '50 Great Guy Meals Even You Can Make'."

Even me? I had to get my hands on that.

"Do I hear two dollars?" Mom asked.

"Why are you starting at two dollars?" I whined. "That's not fair!"

"It's for charity, Vicki. Do you want it or not?"

"Fine. Two dollars."

"Three dollars," my cousin Sarah piped up.

"Four dollars," I said.

"Five dollars," my brother said.

"Wait a minute, Stephen, weren't you the one who donated that book?" I asked.

"Yeah," he said sheepishly, "but now that I see everyone else bidding on it, I realize what a good book it must be."

"Don't bid against me! I'm the one who carried it in from the car! I should have just taken it from the pile before donating it."

"You mean, rob the charity?"

"Ugh, fine. Six dollars."

"Seven dollars," Sarah said.

"Eight." Stephen, again.

"Nine," I reluctantly bid.

"Ten," Sarah offered, counting out her bills.

"Eleven," Stephen said.

"Guys! The book only cost $17 new! Twelve," I bid. This was getting out of hand.

"I only have ten left," Sarah said. "I'm out."

"Thirteen, final offer," Stephen said.

"I'm not paying $14 for a used $17 book," I said.

"I hardly used it," Stephen countered.

"Then stop bidding on it!"

He just shrugged and flashed his $13 at my mom.

"Fine, I'm out. I don't know why I wanted it anyway. They don't even have half of those ingredients in Paris and my suitcase is already jam-packed." Whenever I came home for the holidays, I loaded up on necessities like mac and cheese and pancake syrup, stuff that was near-impossible to find in the City of Light. I wasn't sure this book was worth $14 and precious suitcase space.

"No more bids?" Mom asked. "OK, then. Sold, to the man who donated the book!"

"I'm not sure you understand how auctions work, Stephen," I chided.

"But it was fun, wasn't it?"

The pot had now grown considerably and we were nearly out of books. Mom auctioned off the last few stragglers, then Grandma generously agreed to double the pot.

We flipped through the charity's catalogue and calculated that we could now afford to buy a sheep. It's no water buffalo, but don't tell the sheep that.

We kept this tradition for many years, everyone stockpiling their books throughout the year, excited to trade up for some newbies (Or should that be "usedbies"? No, it shouldn't.) at Christmas. It gave us something to do in a crowded space and ensured that everyone ended up with something they liked, whether that be shirtless men or cyborg aliens or shirtless cyborg aliens.

Christmas Cosmo

The year I snagged the penguin martini shaker and assorted mixes was exhilarating, much like the flavor of this cocktail. You'd be surprised how good a pre-made cocktail mix can be, but of course it's always best to dress it up with a special touch.

lemon wedge
cosmopolitan rimmer mix (or you can use sugar)
3 oz. cosmopolitan mix
2 oz. vodka
splash of cranberry juice

1. Slide the lemon wedge around the rim of the martini glass, then coat with cosmopolitan rimmer mix (or sugar).
2. Pour cosmopolitan mix and vodka into a martini shaker full of ice. Add a splash of cranberry juice for holiday cheer. Shake well.
3. Strain into martini glass, and gloat over your fabulous Christmas gifts.

Makes 1 serving

2

A Hole Lot of Fun

Nothing is more ridiculous than getting Christmas presents for your pets. They don't know what holiday it is. They're not expecting gifts. It's not like they wrote out a wish list with their non-opposable thumbs and are snooping around the tree sniffing each wrapped present to see if their new doggie bone or bejeweled kitty collar is waiting for them. I mean, they do sniff around the tree but that's because they sniff *any* new object that enters the house.

Of course, just because it's ridiculous doesn't mean I don't do it. Part of the reason we give our pets gifts is because we enjoy doing it, regardless of the practicality or necessity. We love watching them play with their toys and wear their new bejeweled kitty collars. It's a lot like giving gifts to your kids, except without all the whining and wails of "We're bored" after ten minutes. No, your pets will play with their toys for hours, days, months and won't ever expect anything more.

For my kitten Penelope's first Christmas, I got her the cutest Garfield stuffed animal. It had a furry body, head, and paws, with thin elastic arms and legs so she could stretch the heck out of it. She loved that thing like it was her own baby kitty. She took him everywhere. Played with him, slept with him, caused loads of trouble with him.

I'd leave for work in the morning, blowing her a kiss goodbye as she sat by the front door wearing her most innocent expression, Garfield propped up just as innocently beside her.

Then I'd come home to see an overturned glass of water and Garfield—the obvious culprit—lying in the puddle.

Or the trash can would be on its side, garbage spread all across the kitchen, with Garfield's guilty paw resting on the trash can lid.

It's like Penelope thought she could get away with blaming it on him. "Me? Oh, no no no. Not me. Clearly it was Garfield who barfed in the corner. Garfield kicked kitty litter outside the box. Garfield took a nap on your bed and left an adorable kitten-shaped indentation in your pillow. Wait no, that last one was me. Aren't I the cutest?" Then she'd bat her eyelashes and start purring and I'd forget what I was mad about.

༄༅

"Isn't it so cute how they amuse themselves?" I asked my brother one day when I had stopped by his house to check out his latest home improvements. This was back when we both still lived in St. Louis, before I embarked on my new life in Paris and before Stephen moved to Michigan to rehab houses. I'd just finished telling him about Penelope's latest antics.

"Totally. Check this out. Chopper plays catch by himself." He grabbed a tennis ball, which immediately attracted his German Shepherd's attention. "Hey Chop, go get the ball!"

Stephen dropped the ball on the floor and Chopper caught it on the first bounce. Then, clearly having done this before, he trotted over to a hole in the floor by the front door. A dessert-plate-sized hole that went all the way down to the basement. How had I missed that when I walked in?

"Why is there a hole in your living room floor?" I asked, which is a question I imagine people don't often ask their brothers.

"You remember that half wall that divided the kitchen and the living room? Yeah, I got rid of that," he replied, with what he clearly thought was a normal answer.

"But what about the hole?"

"Well, I guess it'd been hiding under the half wall." He shrugged, then pointed to Chopper, who dropped the ball down the hole. Then Chopper raced over to the basement steps and thundered down. "Watch," Stephen said, looking through the opening.

Sure enough, we could see Chopper through the gap, fetching the ball before he charged back up the stairs. Next on the agenda: dropping the ball again and repeating the process infinity times.

"He never gets tired of it!" Stephen said. "Hey, want to see my basement?"

If his basement remodel had gone anything like his wall removal, I couldn't wait to see.

We headed downstairs, passing Chopper on the way, who was so intent on his solo game of fetch he didn't notice us, and Stephen showed me the fruits of his labor.

"This here is to hide the furnace," he said, pointing to a passable drywall job.

"How do you get in to change the air filter?" I asked, noticing there was no door to the enclosure.

"Pffft. Air filters. Who needs 'em?"

At this point in my existence, I was shocked at the thought of not having an air filter in my furnace. In later years, after I moved to Paris, I would complain about how Parisian apartments didn't have screens on the windows.

"Mom, it's insane," I said on our weekly long-distance phone call. "How can they not have screens? All sorts of bugs get in, even up here on the seventh floor. How do bugs even get that high?"

"Ew, gross," she predictably replied, detesting insects as much as I did. "I would have thought the bugs would tire out at the fourth or fifth floor."

"I know, right? And don't even get me started on the pollution. Can you believe all that dirty air just blows right into our apartment?"

"Well, I'm not sure a screen would really block much."

"Still, it would block some. It's gross to think about breathing in all that air."

"Yeah, but… what about when you're outside?"

Touché. Obviously I didn't walk around the streets of Paris covered in screens. Maybe I was overreacting.

However, back in St. Louis, in Stephen's basement, my pre-Paris suburban mind couldn't jibe with the thought of not changing the air filter on a regular basis. But more importantly, what if there was a fire? Or required maintenance?

"Oh, don't worry, I've got that covered," he said, with astounding confidence for someone who just drywalled in a furnace that wasn't likely to pass inspection. "See this grate here," he said, pointing to an air vent midway up the wall. "I just unscrew that and climb in."

"Seems like a lot of work. And can you even fit through that vent space? And what happens on the other side? You just tumble down on the floor next to the furnace?"

"You worry too much."

"You don't worry enough!"

He shrugged. "Wanna see the bedroom?"

There was a bedroom next to this fire hazard? Lord help us. "Sure."

We walked over to another passably drywalled wall and he reached for the door handle. Something was off.

"What's wrong with this door?" I asked, not quite able to put my finger on it.

"What? Nothing," he said, opening the door. He spread his arms in a motion meant to indicate "Voilà, look at this amazing room I created."

But I was still stuck on the door. I realized what was bugging me about it. "Why is the handle so low down?"

"Oh, that? Yeah, well, since the basement has a dropped ceiling, the pre-fab door I bought didn't fit. So I just sawed off the bottom."

"Why didn't you exchange the door for one the right size?"

"Too much trouble."

"Shouldn't you have cut it off the top so the handle remained in the same position? Or some off the top and a little off the bottom?"

He paused for a second, and I caught a glimpse of what might have been a look of, "Damn, I didn't think of that," but he quickly recovered with, "Why make two cuts when you can make one?"

"Um, so that people other than Oompa Loompas can open the door?"

"What's the big deal? So what. You have to bend over a bit. Wanna see the room or not?"

"Sure," I said, stepping in and looking around. The

rest of the room was decidedly normal. Of course, it had the standard tiny window that most basements have, too high up to actually crawl out of if, oh, I don't know, the drywalled-in furnace next to you caught on fire. I casually walked out of the bedroom, focusing on keeping my breathing steady instead of conducting the amateur fire safety inspection I so badly wanted to. Maybe I was being paranoid?

We were back in the main basement area now, which was lined with two guitars, a bass, and a drum set. Chopper was still running back and forth fetching his ball. I guess it wasn't so bad after all. I was impressed Stephen had done all the construction himself and created a cool space for his band to practice in, albeit small.

"So, any other renovations planned?" I was almost afraid of the answer, but maybe he'd surprise me.

"Well, you see how it's kind of cramped down here? I'm thinking of replacing the stairs with a spiral staircase. Open it up a bit."

My breath caught in my throat. Fire Safety Inspector was back. I'd tried to overlook the enclosed furnace. Maybe it would never catch on fire in this 50-year-old house. Maybe everyone would luck out. Or maybe a bunch of bandmates and groupies would be hanging out and then bam! Furnace explodes and people scramble to get up the spiral staircase, or fumble with the too-low bedroom door handle and try to squeeze through the too-tiny window.

"Um…" I felt bad criticizing the home improvements he'd been so proud of, but I'd never be able to sleep at night with the image of my baby brother and his friends rushing to escape a burning blaze. "What about Chopper? Don't you think it would be hard for him to get up and down the stairs?" Chopper was enormous, and while I was sure he'd climb Everest if it meant getting his precious tennis ball, I wasn't sure he could manage a narrow, curvy staircase on a daily basis, particularly considering he hadn't stopped fetching the ball since I'd arrived. That was a lot of up and down for a big dog.

"You're right. I hadn't thought of that. Yeah, maybe I'll skip the spiral staircase."

Whew. I didn't want to point out that he should also fix the giant hole in the floor upstairs, because then I couldn't use Chopper playing fetch as my excuse for not installing the Staircase of Death. One thing at a time.

We headed back upstairs and plopped down on his couch, sending tufts of fur flying everywhere. Oh, the joy of pets.

"So, what are you getting Chopper this year for Christmas?" I asked. At the mention of his name, Chopper twitched his ear and padded over to me. I rubbed his huge head as he panted, taking a much needed break from his solitary game.

"As long as I don't fix that hole in the floor, I don't really need to get him anything," Stephen said.

At this, Chopper turned to Stephen with a look like, "Wha??? You no get me gift?"

"But I'll probably get him a few more tennis balls. I'm sure he'd put them to good use."

As for me, I'd be getting my brother a home improvement manual and a gift card to Home Depot.

Hair of the Dog

After a night of crazy drinking, the last thing you want is to drink more. But sometimes having just a taste will ease the hangover. I've only been able to stomach the thought of a day-after drink once, and I admit it helped. Still, brave is the soul who manages alcohol for breakfast when they imbibed their last drop of alcohol only hours earlier.

2 oz. tomato juice
2 oz. lime juice
dash of Worcestershire sauce
dash of Tabasco
1 bottle of light beer
lime wedge

1. Fill a pint glass with ice.
2. Add the tomato juice, lime juice, Worcestershire sauce, and Tabasco. Stir.
3. Top with beer (as much as you feel you can handle) and garnish with lime wedge.
4. Sip s-l-o-w-l-y as you swear you'll never drink this much again. Until the next time.

Makes 1 serving

3

Suck It Up

Arachnophobia is genetic. I looked it up on the internet.

Wait no, that's arrhythmia. And only certain kinds. In any case, I have both and so does my mom.

Growing up, if I heard a sudden, overly dramatic gasp or a blood-curdling scream, it meant my mom had just spotted an eight-legged creature within creeping distance. It would immediately send chills down our spines and we'd freeze in place, a modern-day Pompeii, while we waited for my brother (our resident bug-killer since my parents were divorced) to catch the little bugger.

Stephen had no fear of the critters, so maybe it's a girl thing or maybe it's a case of nurture versus nature. Ew, just saying "nature" makes me think of all the bugs crawling around outside. Excuse me while I double-check that all the doors are locked.

Lest you think my mom and I are being unfair to

arachnids, we detest all creepy-crawlies equally, regardless of the color of their skin or the number of their legs.

I carried this fear with me when I moved to Paris, though I foolishly thought cities didn't have bugs. Cities were far from nature, and nature was where bugs lived. Logical. Can you tell I majored in math in college?

So imagine my surprise and disgust when my Parisian apartment had just as many insects as my suburban home back in St. Louis.

One weekend, while I was living with my then-boyfriend Pierre, I encountered a mutant flying insect. It was the size of a hummingbird, but nowhere near as cute. Its wingspan made it hard to believe this was a bug and not a bird, but the creepiness of its exoskeleton clued me in.

And of course, the weekend this monster decided to fly in my seventh floor window was a weekend when Pierre was out of town.

I was alone with this beast. The two of us would have to fight it out.

At first, I tried to ignore it. That worked for 42 seconds. It flapped its giant wings next to my face, creating a cool breeze that was welcome in the summer heat, except for the fact that it originated from one of Satan's minions.

Only one of us would be able to stay in that apartment. I contemplated crashing at a friend's house for the weekend but I couldn't bear the smug expression on the winged creature's face as he saw me pack my bags in defeat.

I was going to have to kill him. And fast, before I lost my nerve.

I grabbed an innocent piece of paper, which was oblivious to the fact it was about to be used as a murder weapon. I slapped the bug with the paper and continued the deadly motion straight to the wall. It was a quick death. Instant. I felt bad about killing one of God's creatures but I strongly suspected that thing came straight out of hell. It might have even had fangs. The world was a safer place without this guy in it.

I tugged the paper from the wall to survey the damage. It was a blood bath. I won't go into detail (you can thank my editors for that), but suffice it to say, I couldn't leave it like that. I was gagging just looking at it. I couldn't clean it up, either, because I would do worse than gag if I had to actually dispose of the gruesome, splattered body.

So I did the only reasonable thing: I taped the piece of paper to the wall to hide the crime scene.

The rest of the weekend passed without incident. I even managed to forget about the grisly murder I'd committed until Pierre came home.

"Why is a piece of paper taped to the wall?" he asked.

"Welcome back! Good to see you," I said, trying to hide the inevitable under a veil of politeness. It didn't work.

He walked over and flipped up the piece of paper to reveal the bloodied carcass. "Gross!"

"Now you see why I covered it up."

"Why didn't you just clean it up?"

Seriously, didn't he know who he was talking to?

Thankfully he wiped up the mess and we moved on with our lives. Well, not the bug.

୬୦୰

Years later, I married the love of my life, Mika. It would be hard to find a bad quality about this guy. He's patient. He's kind. He's funny and smart. He's a wonderful husband and an amazing father.

But he absolutely sucks at killing bugs.

His technique: Grab a paper towel and stomp loudly

toward the bug, usually scaring it away before arriving on the scene. If the stupid thing sticks around, it's only because he's thinking, "Get a load of this guy and his soft, fluffy paper towel. What's he planning to do with that? Tuck me in to bed and sing me lullabies? Sounds lovely!"

Mika's "plan" is to gently cover the area the spider is occupying, and to—I don't know—just hope the spider crawls into the paper towel's pillowy folds, leading itself to death? Of course the spider darts away each time and now Mika's just wasted a paper towel.

"You have to smash it. With force," I said, with all the knowledge of a backseat driver. "The paper towel is just to protect your fingers from the carnage. You actually need to kill it with your hand."

He gave me a look like, "Holy hell, who did I marry?"

I gave him a look back like, "You better kill the next one or you won't stay married for long."

One week later, I was minding my own business (so, ending world hunger or spending too much time on Facebook) and I heard a loud SMACK in the kitchen.

"Check this out," Mika said, entering the living room with a smile on his face and a dark smear on a paper towel.

Ah, my technique worked.

ڡچ

This doesn't solve my mom's problem, though. My newly-trained bug-killing husband was thousands of miles from St. Louis. My step-dad, Doug, will take care of any insect problem, but what does my mom do if he's not there? She would never kill an intruder herself, but she can't stay frozen in one spot all weekend.

Enter the best Christmas present ever, courtesy of

SkyMall: the bug vacuum.

I'd traveled home for Thanksgiving one year, opting for the cheaper international fares for that time period compared to Christmas. After reading the in-flight magazine cover to cover (or at least taking the Mensa quiz to feel smart), I perused the SkyMall catalogue.

Have you ever looked in that thing? I wanted to buy everything on every page! And I nearly did.

Toy gun that shoots marshmallows? Perfect for my trigger-happy, sweets-loving brother. (Bonus: New way to play fetch with Chopper.)

A glass display case for children's artwork where you slide in their new artwork while cleverly hiding their previous masterpieces so that you don't have a house full of scribbles? Perfect for my colleague who has two adorable, prolific, artistic children.

Collapsible silicone wine glasses that you can—get this—fold up and tuck in to your back pocket so you're ready for any occasion? I might just have to get those for myself.

A bug vacuum with extendable arm and a circular shield to trap the bug before being sucked away to ~~get zapped by a jolt of electricity~~ go live on a farm in the country? Perfect for my easily-spooked arachnaphobic mother. She talks smack about bugs, but can't handle actually smacking any.

Bonus gift: A battery-operated bug-zapping tennis racket for the flying critters. Plus it counts as exercise because it has "tennis" in the name.

I filled out the order form and dropped it in the mail when I landed. Christmas shopping had never been so easy.

Bug vacuum: $64.95

Battery-operated bug-zapping tennis racket: $16.95

Living in a bug-free house: Priceless

Grasshopper

Grasshoppers are one of the most innocuous bugs, which is why I chose this drink for this story. I mean, would you actually drink anything with "spider" or "heebie jeebies" in the name?

1 oz. crème de cacao
1 oz. crème de menthe
1 oz. vanilla vodka
2 oz. half-and-half

1. Fill a martini shaker with ice.
2. Add the crème de cacao, crème de menthe, vodka, and half-and-half.
3. Cover and shake until well-chilled.
4. Check that there aren't any bugs in your martini glass, then strain the liquid into your glass.

Makes 1 serving

4

Père Noël is Coming to Town

"What would Leo like for Christmas this year?" my mom asked over the phone.

"Oh, I don't know. He already has way more than he needs and you know the Lesages are going to spoil him rotten."

"Well I'm his grandma, too! I want to spoil him!"

I was worried about our 16-month-old son, Leo, receiving an overwhelming amount of gifts that would fill our overcrowded apartment to overflowing. And as I was now four months pregnant with Baby #2, I was taking up a decent percentage of the apartment on my own.

"Maybe you can deposit money into his bank account?" I suggested.

We'd opened a bank account for Leo soon after he was born, which entailed even more paperwork than is typical for the French, since each parent had to sign 56 pages of mumbo jumbo.

It was worth it, not only to start my son's savings early but to receive his bank statement in the mail each month, addressed to "Monsieur Leonardo Lesage." I realize that's just French for "Mister Leonardo Lesage" but it still sounds cool. It seems so official for someone who still poops his pants.

"Mommy, could you please pass my earnings statement? I'd like to see how much interest I've accrued. And then I'll need a diaper change. It's a big one."

Clearly I'm easy to please if baby bank statements give me the giggles.

"Sure, I can deposit money into his account," my mom said. "But I want to give him fun stuff, too."

"Maybe you can stock up on toys to keep at your house? He'll need something to play with when we visit."

"Ooh, great idea! I'm gonna take Doug shopping today."

One set of grandparents down, two to go.

Next up, Dad and Marsha. Marsha was my sweet step-mom, who already had a bunch of grandbabies from her own four kids. So when I suggested cash, they were grateful for the simplicity.

Now I only had to worry about Mika's parents (and aunts and uncles and grandparents). Not that I didn't want my son to have new toys and books and whatnot. I just didn't want him to be spoiled.

However, since Leo was Gilbert and Catherine's first grandchild, they couldn't help themselves. Every week when I unpacked the groceries, there'd be all sorts of toys and games amongst the ~~hot dogs and chips~~ asparagus and Brussels sprouts. If this was what happened on a weekly basis, there would surely be an avalanche of gifts under the tree this Christmas. The horror!

༝ঙৎ

"How does this sound?" Mika asked one night after picking Leo up from day care. "Pumpkin soup, smoked salmon, zucchini au gratin, and tiramisu."

"Exquisite. Is that what you're preparing for dinner tonight?" We didn't have any of the ingredients so I was doubtful.

"No, sorry. It's what Leo had at the *crèche* today for Christmas lunch."

"Are you serious? I had a baloney sandwich. This kid eats better than me!"

"I know! I'm jealous."

Our *crèche* had really outdone themselves. Not only were they sure to never repeat the same fruit, vegetable, or meat in one week, but they'd whipped up this masterpiece? We needed to hire the day care chef to prepare our own dinners!

ༀ

Christmas is a few days away!" I said, giddy with excitement. "What kind of cookies do you want to leave out for Santa?"

Mika stared back at me blankly.

"You know... how we leave out milk and cookies for Santa Claus on Christmas Eve?"

Still no clue.

"I know Leo is a bit young but it's an excuse for us to eat cookies!"

"Sorry," he said, snapping out of it. "I was confused. In France we leave out carrots and water. For the reindeer."

No wonder the French are so skinny.

If that was the tradition in the U.S., not only would we have less of an obesity problem, but I might not have ever figured out Santa wasn't real.

Each Christmas, Stephen and I would faithfully set

out cookies and milk, selecting different treats each year so that Santa wouldn't get bored.

"Should we give him Oreos or Pitter Patters?" I asked my four-year-old brother one holiday season.

He pondered the question with the seriousness it deserved. "We got Oreos last year. What about Chips Ahoy? They're the yummiest!"

"Yeah! Mommy, can you please buy Chips Ahoy for Santa?" I asked.

"Sure, honey."

Except she didn't. 'Twas the night before Christmas and all through the house, not a Chips Ahoy was in sight, nor Nestle Tollhouse.

"Mommy, what's this?" I asked, eyeing the plate of Fig Newtons set out next to a glass of water.

"I thought Santa might want something different this year. He'll like it, you'll see."

Nobody liked Fig Newtons except Mom. And water? Who preferred water with cookies when you had the choice of milk? Except for Mom.

Wait a minute...

At six years old, I wasn't 100% positive about my assumption. Plus, I didn't want to sabotage my chance of getting gifts if there really was a Santa Claus. I decided to play along, just to be safe.

The next morning, bountiful presents were packed under the Christmas tree. Whew, Santa had come after all.

But then I discovered a second clue. "Mommy, Santa Claus has the same handwriting as you," I said, pointing to a gift tag.

"What a coincidence!"

"And he liked Fig Newtons and water, just like you."

"Well isn't that funny!"

"Yes, that is funny." I was on to her but didn't want to ruin Stephen's fun.

But he was on to her, too. "Wait a minute, Mommy. Are YOU Santa Claus?"

She was caught red-handed.

If only we had set out carrots and water for the "reindeer," we kids would have never been the wiser. Because if there's one thing Mom likes more than Fig Newtons (and one thing even more boring than Fig Newtons), it's carrot sticks.

ॐॐ

We spent Christmas Eve at Mika's parents' house, opting to set out neither cookies nor carrots since we'd be stuffing our faces at the holiday dinner.

As expected, Leo was showered with gifts from Père Noël. Mika's sister, Adeline, was also Leo's godmother and therefore brought extra gifts. Even her new boyfriend arrived with a sack full of presents.

Leo was in heaven. He could hardly decide where to begin. But once he found the loudest toy (miniature pots and pans from Ikea), he banged on them for two hours straight. Thank you, Adeline.

The next day, while Leo was taking a nap and visions of sugar plums danced in his head, Mika and I organized his toys.

Mika packed a box of the more babyish items to be saved for Baby #2. I bagged up toys for charity. We recycled the books with torn pages.

But we were still left with a mound of gifts. We didn't have room for all these toys in our apartment and we were also concerned it would give Leo sensory overload.

We further divided the toys, planning to stash them in the basement and rotate his selection on a monthly basis.

"I'll take them down," I offered.

"No, no, I'll do it," Mika countered. "No way am I

letting my pregnant wife carry boxes down three flights of stairs. They'll arrest me for spousal abuse."

"OK, but I'll organize it afterward."

"Deal."

Mika was great for brute strength but when it came to organizing, I was the master. I was just pondering starting a spreadsheet when Mika returned from the basement.

"OK, all set," he said.

"Great, I'll be back soon," I said, heading downstairs to the *cave*.

Most Parisian apartment buildings have a *cave* (pronounced "kahv," which sounds way cooler than just "cave") but not every tenant is guaranteed a storage unit. And if you are lucky enough to score one, the cave is usually so creepy you wouldn't even want to use it.

In previous apartments, I rarely had the nerve to enter the cave, and never without Mika. These caves were like a scene from *The Goonies* except without the pirate treasure. Bare dirt floors, ominous shadows, suspicious squeaky noises, and a distinctive musty odor.

Half-convinced I would stumble across a skeleton with a whiskey bottle, I always dashed in and out as quickly as possible, then immediately hopped in the shower to rid myself of the inevitable cobwebs stuck in my hair.

This cave, though, had concrete floors and was swept often. The low ceilings and occasional spider reminded you it was still a basement, but I could handle being down there by myself without freaking out. Our storage unit even had its own light!

I settled in to Operation Organization. Since this was our fifth apartment together, Mika and I had discarded a lot of crap on each previous move. The storage unit contained only luggage, seasonal items, and a stash of newborn clothes sealed in bags. But Leo's new toys would fill up half the space. If we were going to stick to our plan of rotating them out on a regular basis, they needed to be part of an organized system. (I really should have gone for the spreadsheet.)

When I finished, I backed out of the storage unit, ready to head upstairs. But outside of the storage unit, the cave was pitch black.

Crap! The overhead light must have been on a timer. The light from our storage unit was bright, but not quite bright enough to reach around the corner to the stairwell where the main light switch was. I'd have to venture into the dark to flip it on.

All of a sudden, the cave seemed a lot scarier. Every zombie movie I'd ever watched popped into my head. When you're sitting on your couch it's easy to shout, "Just stab him in the brain, dummy! What's the big deal?"

But now that a zombie could jump out of a corner at any moment, I realized it wasn't quite so easy. I could probably take a child zombie or maybe another woman. But what if the zombie was a tall man? How would I reach high enough to stab him in the head? Especially since my only weapon was my set of keys?

I ran as fast as I could to the stairwell and hit the light. Whew, no zombies.

I casually strolled back to the storage unit like the cool Zombie Slayer I was. Who's not afraid of zombies now? Now that the light is on.

I flipped off the switch in our storage unit and locked up before the overhead light had a chance to kick off again. Not that I was afraid of zombies. I just wanted to get upstairs before my son woke up from his nap.

Yeah, that was it.

Chocolate Chip Cookie Martini

No matter what type of cookies you set out for Santa, he's guaranteed to enjoy them. Except Fig Newtons. Those are gonna get you a lump of coal. If you really want some brownie points (or should that be cookie points?), give him this martini.

1 1/2 oz. vanilla vodka
1/2 oz. butterscotch liqueur
1 oz. Irish cream liqueur
2 oz. milk
squeeze of chocolate syrup

1. Fill a martini shaker with ice.
2. Add all ingredients and shake a few times.
3. Strain into a martini glass, and leave out next to a plate of cookies for Santa.

Makes 1 serving

5

The Gift That Keeps on Giving

I've lived in too many Parisian apartments to count (that's not true because I actually *can* count to seven, but it's called exaggeration for a reason). Despite their varied layouts, features, and quirks, all these apartments have one thing in common: They're tiny as hell.

Our current apartment boasts a single bedroom, where all four of us sleep. My husband and I share a double bed, where his size 13 feet dangle off the edge. My daughter, Stella, sleeps in a crib six inches from our bed, which turns making the bed into a pinball game. If I scored points each time my butt bounced off the crib and my thighs bounced off the bed, I'd easily be the Pinball Wizard of Paris.

And Leo sleeps in his big-boy bed (ask him and he'll tell you all about it for forever and ever) just a few paces away from that. Not a snort, sniffle, or fart happens in that room without the rest of the family hearing it. But unless we win the lottery (which will never happen because Statistics 101 taught me not to play), we peas are stuck in this pod together.

And it's about twice the size of all my previous apartments.

The upside is that when I'm hand-mopping the floor (which is the only way to clean up all the stickiness kids get on the floor EVERY. DAMN. DAY.) I start feeling pretty darn happy the apartment is so small. That much less to clean, down on my hands and knees like a modern-day Cinderella, except my French prince has already whisked me away and this is the biggest castle we can afford.

So when well-meaning friends and family give us gifts (the nerve!), it's a struggle to find a place for them. I always accept the gifts with grace and a smile, and usually manage to fire off a thank you note in the following week.

Then the real work begins. Apartment Jenga. What will I get rid of to make room for the new item?

Stuff in really good condition:

Ha, now that I have two kids, not many items fall into this category. But I did offload a few champagne glasses (I suppose I can make do with a modest set of 16) to my sister-in-law when she moved into her new apartment. And I have oodles of baby clothes that my chubby kids only wore once before hulking out of them.

I discovered a French website that resells lightly-worn baby clothes and promises a pretty penny for your old clothes. Deal! I only had to wash, iron, and fold everything, snipping errant threads and buttoning tiny buttons so the goods were in the most presentable shape possible. I hadn't gone to that much effort when my own kids wore the clothes, but I was determined to make a buck.

I made twenty.

Despite having followed the company's strict rules to a T, they managed to find something wrong with nearly every one of my items, thus reducing the payout. When you divided my final takings by the number of hours spent sprucing up the clothes, it was below minimum wage!

Fortunately, soon after I received that pathetic check in the mail, one of my friends announced she was pregnant. Get ready for some un-ironed hand-me-downs!

Stuff in decent condition:

Drop it in one of the numerous charity clothing receptacles dotted around Paris. Bonus: Leo, who is obsessed with garbage and garbage cans, considers it a fascinating excursion. Pulling the handle of the clothing depository is his Disneyland, and hearing the resounding thud as the bag of used clothes falls to the bottom of the cavernous bin is music to his easily entertained ears.

Stuff in crappy condition:

We're talking victims of diaper blowouts, spaghetti dinners, and adventures in chocolate. Clothes that are stained and barely hanging on by a thread. Believe it or not, you can put these in the same bins as the decent-condition clothes. Instead of donating them to needy people (because even the neediest person doesn't need my crappy rejects) or sprucing them up for resale, the charity redistributes them to cleaning supply companies to make mops and rags out of them. Isn't that amazing? So clothes that have suffered a rough life of being covered in poop and food get a new life of... being covered in poop and food. But it's better than going straight to the landfill.

Stuff that's never been used:

Here's where it gets fun. I used to sell stuff on Craigslist, until people got weird. Or, I guess people have always been weird, it just took the weirdos a while to discover Craigslist.

One time, I put a bunch of kitchen utensils up for sale. I took a photo of all of them laid out nicely on a table and set the price at one euro each or eight euros for the bundle, even though there were like 20 items. I figured if someone wanted even just a few they'd go ahead and take the entire bundle off my hands.

Nope.

I kid you not, I had people calling me up to come over and buy a spatula for one euro.

"Would you like the whole bundle for eight euros?"

"Oh, no thank you. I just need the spatula."

"Are you sure? I could give it to you for six. I feel bad you having to cross town just for a spatula."

"Oh no, I don't mind. It'll only take me thirty minutes."

What? Who would travel that far just to get a spatula for one euro?

"Please, I insist. Take the whole bunch. No extra charge."

"No, thank you. I really just want the spatula."

If I would have known earlier about the Underground Used Spatula Market, I would have stocked up on my last trip to Ikea and resold them at a profit.

I sold off the rest of my utensils one by one, but my growing pile of one-euro coins seemed piddly compared to the amount of time I spent managing the complex timetable of when these strangers were planning to swing by. Not to mention the fact that I worked from home and could usually get away with lounging around in my jammies all day. Now I had to shower and get dressed and look presentable, all to sell a spatula for one euro. Not worth it.

But what if you have a brand new salt-and-pepper set? Or a clock with a fork for the minute hand and a knife for the hour hand? Those were worth way more than one euro, but I already had a clock and a salt-and-pepper set. I hated to waste an unopened gift, but it wasn't worth the time to photograph it, post an ad, reply to the 42 emails asking about its features ("Now was that salt AND pepper, or just salt?"), as well as be expected to take a shower and get dressed.

Thus was born the Regifting Shelf. Any item that entered our house that couldn't immediately be put to use took a turn on the Regifting Shelf. I made a note of who gave it to us and when so that I wouldn't accidentally give it back to its owner. It may sound heartless, but we seriously had no space. Our bathroom was so small that when you used the toilet, your knees would touch the door. Our kitchen was so small that only one person could be in there at a time, so if you wanted a glass of water while the other person was cooking, they either had to serve your Royal Highness or back out of the kitchen and let you in.

The Regifting Shelf served us well because there was always an event coming up. Which was good because the Regifting Shelf itself was small (Hello, did you hear me complaining about the size of my apartment? That included the shelves.). So as soon as a new item came in, another one would have to go out.

"Hey, babe," Mika said. "Don't forget we have that housewarming party this weekend."

"Perfect!" I said. "Think they'd like a fork-and-knife clock?"

"Who wouldn't?!?"

Then we'd get a fancy schmancy corkscrew from one of Mika's clients. Onto the Regifting Shelf.

"Hey, it's Anne Marie's birthday this weekend."

"What about that corkscrew and a nice bottle of wine?"

The Regifting Shelf served as our own personal store, one that was open 24/7. Which comes in handy in Paris, where almost nothing is open on Sundays and few stores are open late. *Boulangeries* are almost always open because fresh bread is a basic need in this country (one with which I whole-grainedly agree) but most other establishments close their doors at nightfall on Saturday and don't reopen until Monday or sometimes even Tuesday. If you need a last-minute gift, you're screwed.

Of course, during the holiday season French stores recognize that people might actually want to do some shopping, so many stores open their doors *exceptionnellement* on each Sunday in December leading up to Christmas. Predictably, the stores are packed. So those extra open hours don't even help unless you want to do your holiday shopping on the receiving end of an elbow to the rib cage every 4.2 seconds.

As Yogi Berra would say, "No one even goes there it's so crowded." That includes me.

The Regifting Shelf has saved me many a time. And it has saved many an object from ending up in a landfill, or from filling my already full-to-the-brim apartment.

Is it callous? Maybe. But it's the thought that counts, right? Friends, family, and co-workers thought enough to get us something nice. And we thought enough to make sure it found a good home. In someone else's home.

As any lawyer will tell you, the best defense is to blame your mom.

Note from my uncle who's a lawyer: Don't do that.

Note from my mom: Yeah, don't do that!

So if anyone thinks it's uncouth to find a new home

for a gift that doesn't have a comfortable spot in my 215 square foot apartment, I can only say I learned it from the best.

Mom actually gives fantastic presents that I've never had to regift. But she's stingy with the cards.

It all started during the Christmas of 1990, when I was 10 and Stephen was 8. We'd opened our pile of gifts under the tree and thanked her, content with our spoils. Then Mom handed us each a Christmas card.

"A card?" we asked in unison.

"Open them," she said.

We opened them and obscene (to us children) amounts of money fell out. Woo hoo! Money! We Scrooge McDucked, rolling on the living room floor in what was probably a pile of twenty bucks but felt like a fortune to us.

"Thanks, Mom!" we shouted in unison.

"I figured you were old enough to start getting money along with your gifts. That way you can spend it how you wish throughout the year."

As we tossed the money up in the air and let it rain down, she surely questioned if she'd made the right decision regarding our maturity levels. But the cash was in our possession and it was too late now.

The same thing happened the following year. We opened our gifts, then she handed us our cards.

"Woo hoo! Make it rain!" we said in unison. Clearly we hadn't matured much in the past year.

We hardly looked at the cards, as they were merely vehicles for our mad cash stash.

The next year we repeated what was now becoming a tradition. We opened our gifts, thanked her, and then waited patiently for our money, money, money.

Mom handed us each a slightly worn envelope. We opened them and sure enough, each contained a card and some cold hard cash. But something looked... familiar.

Why yes, wasn't that the same card we'd received the year before?

"Yes, it is," Mom said. "You seem to appreciate the money more than the card so I figured I'd reuse the card."

"Good call," Stephen said, pocketing the dough.

"Yeah, good idea," I chimed in. "Though technically since that move saved you $2.25, you could have passed the savings on to us." Always out for that extra buck, I was.

"Vicki! That's not very polite," Mom said.

"I'm just sayin'."

The next year the envelopes looked even more worn, but they were heavier. What the...?

I'll be darned. She actually put the extra $2.25 in, and the quarter had been what was weighing down the envelope.

"So this really is a tradition now, huh?" Stephen asked. He grabbed a pencil and wrote "Stephn was here."

"You forgot the 'e'," I said.

"No, it's right here. S-T-E—"

"The second 'e', dummy."

"Oh, that? I always forget that. Whatever."

And so it became our family tradition that every year we'd open the same Christmas cards, pull out our cash-plus-$2.25, and make fun of Stephen for forgetting how to spell his own name.

I'm keeping this Christmas spirit alive in my own little family. We regift, reuse, recycle. We're "eco-friendly" as opposed to "cheap." Or at least that's what my lawyer told me to say.

Note from my uncle who's a lawyer: No I didn't.

Glitter and Gold

Getting money for Christmas turned my eyes to dollar signs. "You mean I get presents *and* money?" Life couldn't get any better. Here's a golden, glittery shot to remind you of a time when $20 was a big deal. (So, yesterday.)

3/4 oz. Goldschläger
3/4 oz. golden rum

1. Fill a shot glass halfway with Goldschläger, then top with rum.
2. Shoot it, then swim around in your giant pool of money.

Makes 1 serving

Decorations & Celebrations

Decking the halls, Paris-style

6

O Christmas Tree

The summer after Stella was born, we took a family trip to Belgium. If we had waited until she was born to *book* the trip, we never would have done something so crazy. But we had booked it back when my whale of a butt was parked on the couch on strict bed rest for my final 14 weeks of pregnancy with Stella. Getting out of the house sounded awesome. Getting out of the country sounded amazing. Add in the fact that Mika's parents paid for most of it and I was downright giddy.

When the trip rolled around, we packed the rental car with half the belongings of our tiny Parisian apartment and caravanned behind Catherine and Gilbert (a.k.a. Mamie and Papy, a.k.a Mika's parents) to the small town of Jabbeke. On the drive up, we watched as the rolling French countryside flattened into Belgian plains dotted with electric windmills. The kids dozed in the back seat. It was surprisingly relaxing.

Well, except for that one time when we all nearly died.

You see, in the city, we normally take the Métro. Stella had never even been in a car before. Leo rarely rode in one, other than The Big Saturday Grocery Shopping Trip with Mamie and Papy. People back home are often jealous that I live in Paris. What they should be jealous of is the fact that my husband does all the grocery shopping and takes Leo with him, giving me a few hours of relative peace with only one child trying to rip our house apart at the seams instead of two. Anyway, Mamie and Papy learned long ago that they needed to engage the child safety locks in the back seat.

I had not yet learned this lesson.

We were cruising down the Belgian highway, rehashing the latest season of *Game of Thrones*, making predictions for which of our favorite characters would die next season (our guess: all of them), and the furthest thing from our minds was our not-quite-two-year-old opening the door on the highway. So when Leo OPENED THE DOOR ON THE HIGHWAY we were like, "Holy crap, he just opened the door on the highway!"

Mika kept his cool at the wheel, while I freaked out in the passenger seat. *OK, focus.* I squeezed into the back seat and managed to close the door, temporarily solving the problem. I held the handle with a death grip until I figured out my next move. User's manual. I stretched to grab it out of the glove box while still maintaining my hold on the handle and frantically flipped through the 800-page manual (still shorter than a *Game of Thrones* novel) to figure out a) why the regular locks didn't work and b) how to set up the child safety locks.

Turns out, the locks only worked from the outside. So while the dashboard indicated that all the doors were locked, it really meant we could all still get out but no one could get in. Which is incredibly useful in preventing car jackings along dangerous Flemish highways. Except newsflash: The only dangerous thing on Flemish highways is us and our car door!

I paged through the rest of the manual until I finally found the child lock info. I memorized it and visualized the exact steps to take to put the locks in place. Then Mika pulled over to a dangerously narrow shoulder and I hopped out, feeling the car shake every time a speeding vehicle passed us. I had to act quickly.

Flip, switch, lock. Testing one, two, three times. All set. We were back on our way, no longer a threat to the citizens of Belgium. Now we just had to catch up to Gilbert and Catherine.

Of course, Leo continued to pull the handle the rest of the trip.

ᕮᐤᕬ

We eventually arrived in the quaint village of Jabbeke, population 14,000. We had booked a campsite within walking distance of the town. But I'm no camper so we stayed in the ritzy district of the campground, in a three-bedroom mobile home with running water, a kitchen, and crappy wifi.

And spiders. A whole lot of spiders.

I only spotted three inside the mobile home (only!) but I lost count at eleventy billion just outside. I'm not even exaggerating.

I threw open the curtains in the morning, singing "Oh, what a beautiful morning!" and stopped short when I spotted a spider peering through the glass.

"Oh, don't mind me!" the spider said. "I'm just sitting here with eight—count 'em, EIGHT—legs in my creepy ass web that I spun while you were sleeping. You're not actually afraid of me, are you, wimp? What if

I move this leg right here a little bit? Like this?" *Wiggle, wiggle.* "Does that do it? MWAHAHAHAHA!"

I survived the trip by drinking copious amounts of Belgian beer, which remedies any situation.

A few days into the trip, I figured I should give the great outdoors an honest shot. Become one with nature. After all, I used go on Phish tours and camp out after the concerts so surely I could handle a few Flemish arachnids.

"I'm not afraid of spiders!" I declared. "I'm not going to let those—hiccup—jerks ruin my trip!" The higher alcohol content of Belgian beer had instilled unwarranted confidence in me.

I popped Stella in the baby carrier and took a leisurely stroll around the campground. Our "neighborhood" had relatively few trees, so if I stuck to the center of the paved street, I could avoid contact with any creature possessing eight legs. But then that wasn't very nature-y of me.

I ventured into the more heavily wooded area, where the paved roads turned to gravel, the mobile homes turned into tents, and the spiders turned into huge hairy beasts put on this earth to scare the crap out of me.

Stella was blissfully oblivious, leaning against my chest and peering out at the greenery with that "Whoa, this is new!" look that two-month-olds have because, whoa, everything *is* new.

I, however, was being attacked by spiders. If not physically, then very much so in my overactive imagination. They dangled from spindly webs, taunting me. "Madame, would you like to pass? Right this way," they would whisper in my ear.

The meaner ones shouted "Boo!" as I passed their freshly spun homes. Mika appeared at the end of the wooded path and I hurried to reach him.

"Oh, thank God," I said, hugging him. "There are so

many spiders in those woods, I wasn't sure I'd make it out alive."

"Which woods?" he asked.

"Um, these ones right here," I said, pointing to the tree-lined gravel road. Hrm. I could have sworn there were more trees. There were certainly loads of spiders, though of course the bastards were all hiding now.

Luckily, he didn't press further. "We're about to head to the pool. Wanna come?"

"Yes!" Spiders can't swim, can they?

୯୬ଏ୰

All of this is a very long-winded way of saying that when it comes to Christmas trees, you can sure as hell bet mine are fake. No way am I bringing a spider-bearing live tree into my house. Don't even bother telling me that spiders don't like pine needles or that they won't live on dead trees. You'd have an easier time getting me to swear off wine for a year than getting a real tree into my house.

Wait, no wine? For a whole year? Maybe I was a bit hasty there. Fortunately, I can't imagine a situation where I'd ever have to decide between giving up wine and bringing a Christmas tree into my house.

My first Christmas in Paris, knowing I didn't want anything as dastardly as a fresh, pleasant-smelling, spider-laden tree in my home, I searched for a fake tree. My small apartment couldn't support a normal-sized tree, so I settled on one that was two feet tall. I assembled its plastic branches and decorated it with tiny tinsel and miniature ornaments.

"Looks good to me," Pierre said. Being from Brazil, he wasn't used to real trees either.

Done.

That tree served me for years, and in fact I still have it. However, after stowing it in the *cave*, I'm sure it houses just as many spiders as a real tree, and therefore is not allowed into my home.

The year I was single, after breaking up with Pierre but before meeting Mika, I lived in an even smaller apartment. I'd gone from 400 square feet to 215. Of course, without Pierre's junk all over the place (no, not that junk, gutter-mind) it almost felt like I had more room. But I still didn't have room for a tree. I didn't even have a couch.

People find this hard to believe.

"We'd love to come visit you," my step-sister Sarah said over a crackling phone line. She and her boyfriend wanted to make the trip to Paris. She'd visited before and we'd had a blast, so she was eager to come back. "Could we stay with you? We don't mind sleeping on the couch."

"I wouldn't mind except I don't have a couch."

"You don't have a couch?"

"Nope."

"What do you sit on while you watch TV?"

"I don't have a TV."

I waited while her brain exploded on the other end of the line.

"I know," I said. "It's crazy." I download stuff on my computer (100% legally, in case any law enforcement officials are reading this) and watch it while sitting at my kitchen table. It's actually kind of fun (especially the part about not having to pay for it, for all the non-law enforcement people reading this).

"So… what *do* you have?" She probably thought I didn't even have a pot to piss in. And in fact, some people don't—some Parisians share a communal bathroom down the hall from their apartment. No, *merci*.

"I have a kitchen with two hot plates, only one of which works. A toaster oven, but no toaster and no oven. A mini fridge with an even mini-er freezer. A kitchen table with four chairs, not that there's room for four people. An armoire for my clothes and other stuff. My bedroom literally contains just a bed."

"Not even a night stand?"

"Not even enough room to open the bathroom door all the way."

"Got it. So we'd have to find a hotel."

"Yep. But be prepared. Those are small too."

So there wasn't room for a Christmas tree, not even one that was only two feet tall. But it's not Christmas without a tree, right? So I put the darn thing up anyway, and bumped into it anytime I did anything, like blinked or thought about what to cook for dinner on my one functioning hot plate.

The following year was the first Christmas I'd be spending with Mika. We didn't officially live together, but he was over all the time. He's 6'4" and clumsy as a puppy. On a good day, he only knocked over half the stuff in my apartment. So there was no way my elfin tree could share space with my tall, dark, and handsome boyfriend.

"You're not going to put up a tree?" Mika asked. "What a shame!" His big, round puppy dog eyes looked guilty, like he knew it was partly because of him.

"Meh. I tripped over it all the time last year. We're better off without it." I hoped I had convinced him it wasn't a big deal.

But ever the kind soul, he found a solution.

He came over one night in early December bearing an oddly shaped, lightly wrapped package.

"What's this?" I asked, kissing him at the threshold. Ooh, maybe I could get some mistletoe? Or *gui* as they say in French, not that I would ever be able to actually say such a funny-looking word. Gooey? Geee? Gwee?

"You'll see," Mika replied, a huge grin spreading across his adorable face.

What? Oh yeah, a present! I gently pulled back the

tissue paper to reveal... a bonsai tree. No way!

"See? It'll fit right here on the table."

"It's perfect," I said, giving him another kiss. Looks like we wouldn't be needing any mistletoe.

৽৵

"*Aie! Merde!*" Mika shouted, bumping his thigh on the corner of the kitchen table for the trillionth time.

"It's a good thing we didn't set up the Christmas tree, huh?" I said. "It's a tight enough squeeze around here as it is."

"We need a smaller table. This is getting ridiculous."

So we did what every crazy-in-love new couple does: We went to Ikea.

A trip to Ikea is Test #1 of Couple Survival Skills. It doesn't matter if your list only contains two items and you plan to "just be in and out." You will get sucked into the store's inner vortex, and you will leave with 25 more items than you planned. You will be a shell of your former self, but damn if you didn't get a good deal.

We found the perfect table, and it was even on sale, a rare occurrence for Ikea. On the way to the checkouts we passed the Christmas display. And lo and behold, they had ornaments so petite it was like they were made for my bonsai tree! But of course. I wasn't the only Paris-dweller with a miniscule apartment.

We tossed the pack of ornaments in the cart and checked out. Not a single fight or soul-sucking experience the whole trip.

৽৵

"That was the world's easiest trip to Ikea," I said on the ride back.

"I know, we're amazing."

We couldn't be more smug. We were, as the French would say, "throwing flowers at ourselves."

Well done, here's a rose! We're amazing, here's a tulip. We are the happiest, most agreeable couple alive, here's every bouquet on Planet Earth!

Then came time to put the table together. Test #2 of Couple Survival Skills.

"OK, next up we need four screw thingies that look like this," I said. I was the self-appointed project manager on this task. Up to this point, things had gone smoothly. I called out the instructions and we both put the table together. Mika did most of the heavy lifting, not because he's the man and I'm the woman, but because it meant he didn't have to bother with the instructions.

"I only see three," he said.

"Well, we need four." My tone was starting to get snippy, even though it's not like Mika had eaten the screw when I wasn't looking. Had he?

We rummaged around some more. Still no luck.

"This makes no sense. It has to be here. The apartment isn't *that* big."

More rummaging. We knocked heads under the table, as if in a romantic comedy. Except I wasn't laughing. I was pissed off. Where the hell did the screw go? I paid good money for this table. Or, well, I paid money for this table. How could they get away with not giving me all the pieces?

"This is bullshit!" I yelled. "What can we do? Not that I would go all the way back to stupid Ikea, but even if I did, I doubt they would give me a new table. They would just accuse me of losing the screw."

"Looks like we're screwed," Mika said with a smile.

"Yes, that's exactly what we're—oh, I see what you did there."

He smiled again and pulled me to him. We didn't knock heads this time. "Let's take a break and decorate the bonsai tree. We'll figure out the table later."

I didn't want to take a stupid break. I didn't want to figure out the stupid table later. The stupid atypical screws would be impossible to replace and the whole stupid table was probably a waste. Parts were scattered across the kitchen floor. I just wanted to wrap up the project and put it behind me, not decorate a stupid not-even-real-sized Christmas tree.

Wow, was I really that big of a Grinch? Here I had a romantic French guy who just wanted to cuddle and celebrate Christmas, and all I could think about was assembling the table.

He was right. We should decorate the tree. I found the tiny pack of tiny ornaments at the bottom of the trademark blue Ikea sack, and we delicately hung them on the bonsai's tiny branches. We sat on the floor, Mika leaning against the wall, me leaning against Mika, and admired our work.

"Joyeux Noël," he said.

"Merry Christmas," I said.

Our table may have only had three legs, but we'd passed the Ikea Couples Test with flying colors.

The Bonsai

By far the tiniest tree I've ever decorated, my bonsai with cherry-sized ornaments was perhaps also the prettiest. This shot captures the spirit of the East as well as being miniature, like my Christmas tree.

3/4 oz. sake
3/4 oz. green tea (chilled)
maraschino cherry

1. Pour the sake and green tea into a shot glass.
2. Shoot it, then eat the cherry (an edible "ornament").

Makes 1 serving

7

Fortune Cookie

I've always been a big fan of fortune cookies. Obviously I like the fortunes, and the age-old joke of adding "in bed" to the end of each fortune never gets old.

"A special surprise awaits you." (In bed.)

"Advice, when most needed, is least heeded." (In bed.)

"In order to take, one must give." (In bed.)

"Soon life will become more interesting." (In bed.)

I could do this all day.

"The harder you work, the luckier you get." (In bed.)

OK, I'll stop now. But speaking of work and luck, let's talk about France and their absurdly lax work schedule (that I'm lucky enough to benefit from since I work in a French office.)

By law, salaried employees receive five weeks of vacation, but it's not uncommon to receive nine or even eleven weeks, particularly for those who've been with the same company for a long time or who work for large French mainstays. In the summer, small businesses can shut their doors for three weeks straight, leaving only a hastily scrawled note taped to the door indicating their return date. *Boulangeries* thoughtfully provide a list of other bakeries in the neighborhood, lest you be stranded baguette-less in the street.

Offices remain open during July and August, but with a meager workforce. Even if people don't take their entire five weeks in the summer (opting for a more modest month-long stretch), you'll find that at any given time, only about half the staff is present.

This, among other uniquely French customs, affects the entire work year.

Let me break it down for you.

In January, everyone wishes their friends, family, acquaintances, neighbors, butchers, bakers, and candlestick-makers a happy new year.

"I wish you health, happiness, and good fortune for the entire year, and best of luck with all your personal and professional endeavors." (In bed.)

It's a freaking mouthful.

"*Bonjour*, Sophie," I said to our office manager on January 2. "Happy New Year. Do you have a minute to talk about the TPS report?"

"*Bonjour*, Vicki! I wish you health, happiness, and good fortune for the entire year, and best of luck with all your personal and professional endeavors." (In bed.)

"Uh... *oui*, of course. You too. So, the TPS re—"

"And I hope you had a wonderful holiday and wish you nothing but the best for the coming year."

I wished nothing but to finish the damn TPS report. I can't help it. The American workaholic in me would rather cross tasks off a to-do list than engage in an endless exchange of polite-yet-trite phrases, but I figured

I should play the game.

"And you as well, Sophie. I wish you health, happiness, and good fortune for the entire year, and best of luck with all your personal and professional endeavors." (In bed.)

I made it through the morning, enduring this conversation with nearly half of my 40 colleagues. I didn't get a lick of work done and then before I knew it, it was lunchtime.

I headed out to the local *boulangerie*, where the head baker knows me and always starts preparing my *jambon* and *fromage* sandwich when she sees me arrive.

"*Bonjour*, Madame!" she said, not moving a muscle. Maybe they were out of ham and cheese?

"*Bonjour*, Madame," I said. "I'll have the usual."

"Of course. But first, I wish you health, happiness, and good fortune for the entire year, and best of luck with all your personal and professional endeavors." (In bed.)

My stomach growled. "Merci, Madame. And you too."

She gave me a look as if to say, "That's all? I expect at least two more minutes of traditional *politesse* before I make your sandwich."

My stomach roared. Clearly it was even more polite than I was. So I caved. "I wish you health, happiness, and good fortune for the entire year, and best of luck with all your personal and professional endeavors." (In bed.)

Sandwich in hand, I swung by the pharmacy on the way back to the office. All of this well-wishing was giving me a headache.

"*Bonjour*, Madame," the gray-haired pharmacist said.

"*Bonjour*, Monsieur," I replied with the biggest smile I could muster against my pounding head. "I'd like a package of—"

"Happy New Year! I wish you health, happiness, and

good fortune for the entire year, and best of luck with all your personal and professional endeavors." (In bed.)

"Thanks. And you as well. I'd like a package of—"

"I hope this year brings you nothing but the best."

"*Merci*. I hope the same for you. I'd like a package of—"

"And I hope you're not already sick? Maybe another round of wishes will help. I hope sickness stays far from you and your family this year, but if it does show up, I'll be here to help." (In bed.)

I could hardly get mad at a sweet man like this, but for the love of God, I was getting buried under these wishes.

"So what can I get for you today, Madame?"

"Three packages of paracetamol, *s'il vous plaît*." That should get me through the afternoon.

I survived the rest of the day. Thankfully, some of my colleagues were still on vacation so I didn't have to go through the motions with everyone. Just 35 of them.

You have until the end of January to share your good wishes for the year, so it's not uncommon to be stopped by a colleague on January 28th and have to stand there for five minutes while they politely run through their little song and dance.

You've gotta credit the French, though, for their impeccable memory. They always remember who they've exchanged greetings with and who they still need to wish well. That's a lot to remember over the course of thirty-one days.

Combine new-year-wishing with the morning ritual of *la bise* (kissing each of your 40 co-workers on each cheek) and you've used up all of January just being polite.

February is when the real work starts, maybe because they know they only have 28 days of it.

The French give it all they've got (for the requisite 35 hours per week, that is) until May, which is jam-packed with holidays. May 1ˢᵗ is Labor Day and one week later is World War II Remembrance Day, which commemorates the end of the war in Europe. Falling on different dates, but often in May, are the religious yet nationally observed holidays of Ascension and Pentecost Monday.

If a holiday falls on a Tuesday or Thursday, the French will usually *faire le pont* ("make the bridge") and take off the corresponding Monday or Friday to make a long weekend. Depending on how the days fall, you could have nearly half the month off.

In June, knowing everything's coming to a halt soon, employees are averse to beginning any new projects. But they will diligently wrap up existing projects (of which there are many, since no one did jackshit in May).

Any attempts at progress during July and August are futile since no one else is in the office. You can't schedule meetings because there's no one to meet with. And you can't make any decisions until you meet with these people. It's a good time to dust off your shelves, clean out your inbox, and savor an extra cup of *café*.

September is one of the best months to be in France. Fresh energy abounds as everyone is rejuvenated from vacation. They'll kick off projects, make decisions, and get the ball rolling. Invigorating!

They keep this momentum through the middle of November, but as soon as the first Christmas decorations go up, their productivity goes down. For the rest of the year, it's party-planning-this and holiday-shopping-that.

Adding it up, you've got about six good months of work. Half a year.

"All your hard work will soon pay off." (In bed.)

Well, at least there's that.

Lucky Charm

This New Year, I wish you nothing but the best. In fact, I wish you health, happiness, and good fortune for the entire year, and best of luck with all your personal and professional endeavors. (In bed.)

4 oz. lemon vodka
6 oz. pineapple juice
a few splashes blue curaçao liqueur

1. Pour ingredients into a martini shaker filled with ice.
2. Then pour into two cocktail glasses (no need to shake) and enjoy with that special someone. (In bed.)

Makes 2 servings

8

Bedtime Timeline

The excitement and anticipation of New Year's Eve ebbs and flows as we get older. As kids, we couldn't wait to stay up late, even though we'd fall asleep in puddles of drool before the countdown began. As twenty-somethings, we lived it up, partied hard, and didn't go down 'til the sun came up. Once we have kids of our own, we slowly regress to childhood. We're more likely to be passed out on the couch before midnight than wearing out our vocal cords karaokeing until dawn. If we're up in the wee hours of the morn it's because our kids woke up from a nightmare or a diaper blowout or a nightmarish diaper blowout.

The math nerd in me really wants to graph the progression over the years, plotting data points of hours spent partying past midnight vs. years of age. But since I want you to laugh rather than have painful flashbacks of high school math class, I offer you this New Year's Eve

Timeline instead:

Age 0-3

Desired bedtime: What's a "bedtime"? I wake Mommy and Daddy up at all hours of the night, but never the same hours. Keeps 'em on their toes.

Actual bedtime: 8:00 p.m., not counting the 42 middle-of-the-night wake-ups.

Activity of choice: Listening to "just one more" soothing lullaby to lull me to sleep.

Drink of choice: Warm milk.

Age 4-8

Desired bedtime: Never! Life is too fun to sleep! I want to stay up ALL NIGHT LONG!

Actual bedtime: 10:00 p.m. I tried to stay up, but life is too fun and I wore myself out!

Activity of choice: Listening to "Rudolph the Red-Nosed Reindeer" on repeat until Mommy's head explodes.

Drink of choice: Soda, if Mommy lets me, otherwise milk. (And cookies? Please, please, oh pretty please cookies?)

Age 8-12

Desired bedtime: 12:30 a.m. Mom won't let me stay up later anyway, so I'll save my bargaining chip for something more important.

Actual bedtime: 12:30 a.m. I am quite agreeable at this age. Mom's happy she's finally getting eight hours of sleep per night. I heard her say she wishes I would stay this age forever.

Activity of choice: Anything cute and silly. I'm easygoing.

Drink of choice: Soda. Mom lets me have it now since I'm pretty good most of the time.

Age 13-17

Desired bedtime: Bedtime? Seriously? Like, are we really having this conversation? My friends don't even *have* bedtimes. Don't embarrass me. Actually, don't embarrass *yourself*, Mom.

Actual bedtime: 2:00 a.m. All that attitude and eye-rolling took its toll.

Activity of choice: Hanging out with friends instead of my dorky family.

Drink of choice: Vitamin water or kale smoothies or whatever's cool these days. Not that I care what's cool. I'm too cool for that.

Age 18-20

Desired bedtime: 4:00 a.m. It's party time! No parents! College rocks!

Actual bedtime: 4:00 a.m., though it really should have been earlier. Tomorrow's gonna be rough.

Activity of choice: If Mom's reading, Soda Pong. If not,

Beer Pong.

Drink of choice: If Mom's reading, soda. If not, cheap keg beer.

Age 21-29

Desired bedtime: 30 minutes after the last bar closes.

Actual bedtime: An hour after the last bar closes (had to stop off for greasy fast food to stave off a hangover).

Activity of choice: Raging at a club all night, followed by a nightcap at a late night bar. Dancing on tabletops optional but strongly encouraged.

Drink of choice: All of them.

Age 30-39

Desired bedtime: 30 minutes after the kids go to sleep.

Actual bedtime: An hour after the kids go to sleep. Tried to stay up and be cool, but fell asleep on the couch in a puddle of drool.

Activity of choice: Sleeping.

Drink of choice: Water.

Age 40+

Desired bedtime: Who knows? Maybe I'll shoot for midnight once the kids are older and aren't wearing me out every second.

Actual bedtime: Who knows? Depends on how much the kids wear me out.

Activity of choice: Getting together with friends? Watching the ball drop? Counting down and then kissing my husband? Spending an entire night without getting thrown up on by the kids? I really haven't thought this far ahead because the kids are wearing me out.

Drink of choice: Wine, beer, moonshine, anything that's wet and has alcohol. Mama is finally ready to live it up!

I'd like to say I'll give staying up until midnight an honest shot this year, but I'm exhausted just thinking about it. Call me in a few years and we'll see about meeting up for the countdown. In the meantime, I'm gonna fall asleep in about 10, 9, 8... zzz.

After Midnight

If you're staying up until midnight (or anywhere close), you'll need a pick-me-up. The rum and milk might put you to sleep, but the coffee liqueur will balance it out. Hopefully.

2 oz. coffee liqueur
1 oz. rum
2 oz. milk

1. Pour ingredients into a martini shaker filled with ice.
2. Then pour into a cocktail glass (no need to shake) and enjoy until the wee hours of the 'morn (or as late as you can stay up).

Makes 1 serving

Will Work For Food

Office holiday party antics and bizarre French cuisine

9

The Pretzel Shack

You're strolling through the mall, squeezing in some last-minute holiday shopping. Harried customers bump you with their bags, but you don't care. It's the most wonderful time of the year!

Christmas songs are piping through the sound system and cheerful decorations adorn the normally bland support beams of this suburban shopping behemoth.

Could it get any better?

The smell of cinnamon sugar soft pretzels wafts through the air.

Oh yes, it could get better. It could get a lot better.

You wander over to the gem of a store, prepared to turn over your life's savings for a fresh-out-of-the-oven creation and some ice-cold lemonade. Then you notice the mile-long line snaking around the mall.

Your hopes will not be dashed. You will wait in that line, dammit. You will get your soft pretzel, dammit. It's worth 45 minutes of your time. You can review your kids' lengthy wish list, chat with your shopping partner, and dream about the goodness that awaits you once you finally make it to the front of the line.

And once you arrive at the front of that serpentine queue, who will greet you?

Me. Seventeen-year-old me. I will be nice when I say "Welcome to The Pretzel Shack, how may I help you?" but don't be alarmed if I look like a zombie.

Because, you see, after the longest 45 minutes of your life, you get to enjoy a glorious gooey pretzel made with love, just for you. You get to return to your Christmas shopping. You can even sit down if you like.

But me? I've got another 7 hours and 15 minutes before my shift is over.

Not that I'm complaining. I'm just explaining the dead-eyed stare.

I had been working at The Pretzel Shack for a few months by the time Christmas rolled around. I loved the place. I adored the place. I never wanted to quit working at the place.

I was saving up for Spring Break in Hawaii. While most of my classmates were heading to Mexico to drink their asses off and spend loads of their parents' money, my mom had flat-out refused to let me go. No, I could not go on an unsupervised trip to another country. And no, she would certainly not sponsor it. However, my best friend Holly saved the day. She and her dad were going to Hawaii and said I could come with them as long as I covered my costs.

Supervised trip with no alcohol? Check.

All-expense-paid vacation to Hawaii? Well, I was working on that part since all expenses would be paid by me.

Each day in The Pretzel Shack brought me that much closer to my dreamy beach vacation, one I would appreciate since I'd worked so hard for it. Or at least I'd better appreciate it. What if Hawaii sucked? Hawaii didn't secretly suck, did it? Regardless, I'd already told Holly I was in, so now I had to scrounge up enough cash to pay my part.

Aside from needing the paycheck from The Pretzel Shack, I truly loved working there. You know how people in the food industry often say they would never eat where they work? Either they're sick of the food or, more likely, once they've seen the inner workings of the sausage factory they can't stomach the thought of actually consuming food that had been prepared there.

That's not true of the blue-and-white pretzel palace. The place was immaculate. The food was fresh. The teenaged employees actually cared about the customers. We took pride in serving you a fresh lemonade and a piping hot pretzel, flavor of your choice.

As an employee I was allowed to eat as many pretzels as I wanted, and I did. I'd start with a cinnamon sugar pretzel for breakfast, follow up with a salted pretzel with cheese dip for lunch, and finish the afternoon with a sugar-glazed pretzel. And wash it all down with the sugariest, deliciousest lemonade on the planet.

I still salivate just thinking about it. That place was heaven.

And I usually enjoyed serving our customers. My co-workers fought over who got to make the pretzels, which was an admittedly admirable role—have you seen them? Rolling, flipping, dipping those pretzels just for you?

But I preferred the cash register. I was super quick at it and the numbers geek in me had memorized the most common prices (pretzel + soda, pretzel + lemonade, pretzel + dip... great, now I'm in the mood for a pretzel). I'd shout out the customer's total as I gathered their order and would have them cashed out, pretzel in hand, before they even knew what hit them.

I prided myself on the speed with which I exchanged money for carb-laden awesomeness. Cold hard cash for a warm tasty treat.

You'd get the occasional idiot who didn't know how to order, and of course we'd all make fun of him once he was gone, but we'd help him while he was there, ensuring he left with a smile and a pretzel, and no hint of attitude from us.

During the holiday season, though, I had no time for morons who couldn't make up their mind. Not when my line was two miles long and they'd already had 45 minutes to figure out what they wanted.

"Hi! Welcome to The Pretzel Shack," I said, full of holiday cheer. "What can I get for you today?"

"Uh, yeah, I'd like a pretzel and a drink."

Oh really? Well, I left my mind-reading glasses at home today so could you help me out a little? What kind of pretzel? We have nine different flavors. What kind of drink? We have lemonade and six types of soda, all available in three different sizes. Any preference for any of the above?

But instead I replied nicely, as I was paid to do. "An original pretzel and a medium Coke, sir?"

"Uh, yeah, that'd be great. Er, no, make that a large," he said, after I'd scooped ice into the medium cup.

Just breathe. "Of course, sir."

Next customer. "Hi, yeah, I'll take three."

Three, what? Three hot air balloons? Three slaps across the face? Oh, three pretzels. Well then why didn't you just say that? In our customers' defense, we had a 3-for-2 deal, so people tended to buy three. So yeah, I could guess that this lady wanted three pretzels. But again I ask, what *kind* of pretzels? And for all I know, she could be mega-parched from her holiday shopping and want three large sodas. If she would order nouns instead of adjectives, this would go a lot faster.

"Three original pretzels, ma'am? Or would you prefer a different flavor?"

She looked up at the overhead menu as if for the first time, as if it had teleported in once she reached the counter but hadn't been in plain sight the entire time she'd been waiting in line. Her eyes turned to saucers as they fell on the nine options in front of her. Panic set in. She was alone, yet here she was ordering three pretzels. Either she wanted them all for herself (girl, I *totally* get that) or she had two kids running around and she forgot to ask what flavor they wanted. She couldn't risk losing her place in line to ask them, but she clearly didn't want to risk bringing back the wrong kind.

"Let me guess, ma'am. One is for you and two are for your kids?"

"Yes," she said, her relief palpable.

"Then how about let's get you an original and then two cinnamon sugars for the kids? Throw in a few dips and lemonades and you're all set."

"THANK YOU." She looked like she wanted to kiss me.

I might not have had a white beard or a red hat, but I did give people what they wanted. And I did have a belly that jiggled like a bowl full of jelly, but what did I expect living on a diet of pretzels and lemonade?

Hour after hour, I kept the smile glued to my face and helped customer after customer enjoy a scrumptious break from their Christmas shopping. The rote tasks became part of my body, as if I was born to handle pretzel tongs and punch numbers into the till. I sold those pretzels as fast as they shot out of the oven. My line was always long, but not because I was slow. It was because people kept coming back for more.

When my shift finally ended, I headed home to sleep the day off. But restful, it wasn't. Talk like Yoda, I do.

You see, all night long, for the same eight-hour

length as my shift at The Pretzel Shack, I dreamed about helping customers. I ran through the list of flavors. Recounted the price difference between a medium and large soda. Asked if my dreamland customers wanted a marinara sauce with their garlic pretzel. Counted out their one dollar and 31 cents change and handed it to them, coins first, then bills, before wishing them a happy holiday.

I woke up the next morning and prepared to spend another day of my winter break earning cash and serving pretzels. It was hard to face the thought of eight straight hours helping customers when I'd just done that the previous day and felt like I'd done it the entire night, too. And braving the Christmas-season mall parking lot was no joy either.

But I knew a cinnamon sugar pretzel was waiting for me, right next to a cup of hot coffee. Pretzel Shack, here I come.

The best part? Even (mall) Santa himself stopped by for a pretzel. And in case you're wondering, Mr. Claus likes an original pretzel with salt, a cheese dip on the side, and a medium Coke. I went ahead and gave him a large. Christmas was fast approaching, and it couldn't hurt to get on the old man's good side.

Cinnamon Cider Sensation

In tribute to the always-appetizing cinnamon sugar pretzels at The Pretzel Shack, here's a sweet recipe to get you in the holiday spirit.

30 oz. apple cider (non-alcoholic)
5 oz. dark rum
5 oz. cinnamon schnapps
1 Red Delicious apple, for garnish

1. Pour the apple cider, dark rum, and cinnamon schnapps into a large pitcher. Stir.
2. Fill glasses with ice and top with the spiked cider.
3. Garnish with apple slices, and enjoy the cinnamon-y, sugary goodness.

Makes 8 servings

10

A Crisis of Faith

*We cordially invite you, Monsieur and Madame Lesage, to
Christmas Eve dinner at our house.*

Would you look at that! A formal invitation for our
first Christmas as a married couple. Mika and I had only
been married for a few months at that point, so the
novelty of being called "Madame" instead of
"Mademoiselle" hadn't worn off yet, and my new last
name still sparkled and shined. Partly because Mika's aunt
had gone overboard with the glitter on her handcrafted
invitation.

Catherine, Gilbert, and Adeline swung by to pick us
up, and we headed out to the suburbs for the party. As
we rounded the first turn, a loud clang emanated from
the trunk.

"What's that?" I asked.

"Champagne," Catherine answered. Mika's aunt and
uncle, Martine and Philippe, would provide snacks,

appetizers, the main course, and dessert. All we had to do was sit back and stuff ourselves. "I didn't want us to show up empty handed. I got a bottle for each of us." My kind of lady. "And it's already chilled." Totally my kind of lady.

With the traffic getting out of Paris, it took nearly an hour to get to Martine and Philippe's house. When we arrived, we saw that all the other guests had beaten us there. That meant nearly another hour of saying hello to everyone, since Mika's family gives not two but four cheek kisses in greeting. And then you've got the "*Bonjour*, how are you" bit and a brief recap of the latest and greatest in each person's life. Save something for the party, guys!

Finally, Martine took our not-quite-as-chilled champagne and showed us to our seats. The fourteen of us filled her dining room to capacity. All the kids had to sit on stools since there weren't enough chairs. That included me, even though I was 31 years old. I should have been flattered, but I really just wanted a back to my chair. The stool would be comfortable for about the first five minutes, then it would be hell. At least we had champagne!

"OK, everyone!" Philippe said, standing at the head of the table. "What'll you have to drink? We have wine and whiskey." And... champagne?

"Um, I guess I'll have wine," I said, giving Catherine a surreptitious look. Maybe they were saving the champagne for later? I shrugged. I could start with wine.

"Me too," Catherine said.

Philippe opened the wine painfully slowly and poured even more slowly. Then he continued around the table taking everyone's drink order. Catherine hadn't yet taken a sip of her wine, so I gathered that we should wait until everyone was served before starting. All fourteen of us. The party girl in me was dying. I could have polished off two glasses in the time it took Philippe to serve everyone!

"And what'll you have, Mika?" he asked, at last completing his tour around the table.

Mika wasn't a big fan of wine—shocking, I know. Is he sure he's French?—so I knew he'd go for the whiskey.

"Whiskey and Coke please."

"What?" Philippe bellowed. "That's sacrilege! You can't mix this fine whiskey with Coke. Here, let me serve it to you straight."

He placed one lone ice cube into a glass and poured a huge dose of whiskey on top. "Here, it'll put hair on your chest."

Ew! I liked the minimal amount of hair Mika already had on his chest. But I didn't waste time worrying about my husband turning into Bigfoot because now everyone had finally been served. Time to drink!

"Time for a toast!" Philippe said.

Oh, right. He gave a mercifully short toast, and then it was time to clink glasses. Another tradition, this one almost as torturously long as the four-kiss hello. You have to clink glasses with each person at the table (not one big huddled mass like you can get away with in the U.S.) and you have to look them in the eyes when you do it or else it's bad luck. And you can't cross arms either, like, you can't reach over the person next to you to get to the thirteenth person across from you or else it's bad luck. So instead of enjoying your drink, you had to endure another hour of being absurdly polite, keeping track of superstitions, and carefully avoiding any breaches of etiquette.

It's actually a good thing Martine hadn't served our champagne or it would have been room temperature by then.

Once everyone had properly cheers-ed and clinked, I settled onto my stool and took my first sip. I'd thought it would taste glorious by now, but my stomach was feeling a little weird. Maybe it was because my back was killing me from the stool. And I felt a headache coming on. I nursed the lukewarm glass of wine until the first course was served.

ॐ∽

I remember the first course being delicious, but I don't remember what it was. My back was murdering me and my headache was in full force.

My cousin Florian, Martine and Philippe's son, had prepared the *entrée*[1]. He was in culinary school and this was his first event. He proudly presented the dish and everyone clapped. Now my headache was really pounding.

Everyone raved over how excellent the dish was. I cleared my plate. My back still hurt.

"More wine?" Philippe asked.

"No, *merci*," I said. Who was I? Where had Party Girl gone?

I'm sure the main course was delicious as well, but to me it tasted like Broken Back on Wooden Stool. Which is what my Native American name would totally be. Though if I was a Native American, I probably wouldn't be stuck on a stool in a cramped apartment in a Parisian suburb. I'd be more like Smokes Peace Pipe on Teepee Floor. I could really go for a toke on the ol' peace pipe right about now. You know, for medicinal purposes.

---

[1] Ready to get confused? In French your *entrée* is your appetizer and your main course is your *plat*. So, the exact opposite of how we say it in the U.S., where your main course is called your entrée and your appetizer might be referred to as a "plate" or "small plate" depending on the hoity-toityness of the restaurant you're at. My appetizers are usually called "a basket of everything you can deep fry" but that's another story.

My discomfort had gotten to the point where it was all I could think about. I'd switched from wine to water and couldn't get enough of the stuff. I was hoping to drown the headache, but so far it wasn't working. On the upside, it gave me an excuse to go to the bathroom frequently, and thus stretch my legs during the short walk down the hall.

Around midnight, dessert was served. At last they busted out the champagne, along with two *bûches de Noël*, traditional sponge cakes that look like Yule logs. They're really cute and taste much better than they sound. I managed a piece (please, I can have the biggest headache and I still won't turn down dessert) and a few sips of champagne.

I toasted Catherine, both of us thrilled we could finally dip into the bubbly. But I dreaded toasting the other twelve people, lest my prized drink lose its chill. Fortunately, everyone else's enthusiasm had dwindled as well, so no one was monitoring my manners.

We ate in relative silence, everyone in a food coma and/or wincing with pain at being stuck on a stool for so long. We were wrapping up a marathon eight-hour meal. Actual marathons took less time to finish.

"OK, now it's time for presents!" Martine trilled, after she had cleared the last dessert plate.

Ooh, presents! I'd nearly forgotten about those. And maybe we'd finally get to move to more comfortable seats. Like in the living room. But wait a minute. Where *was* the living room? I didn't recall passing it on the way to the bathroom. I looked around the dining room and realized that while it was small for fourteen people, it was quite large for a French apartment. Uh oh. This *was* the living room. And dining room. In one. Looks like we wouldn't be changing seats after all.

Martine and Philippe played Santa and handed out the gifts, and everyone tore everything open in one go. It was a frenzy like I'd never seen. Even at my grandma and grandpa's crazy-full house, we let each person linger over opening their gifts, allowing ample time to ooh and ahh. "Ooh, I've always wanted reindeer socks!" "Ahh, a reindeer sweater to go with the socks!" You showed your appreciation (real or manufactured) to the gift-giver, then the next person took their turn.

But this scene was straight out of a cartoon, where everyone ripped shreds of paper off their gifts like there was a million dollars inside, sending red and green paper shrapnel flying in the festive air. I couldn't even see what each person had received before it was all over.

"Well, I guess we better get going," Gilbert said. A city dweller to his core, he didn't often drive. So he really didn't like driving at night. The plan was to stay next door at his parents' house and leave first thing in the morning. So, in a few hours.

We filled our arms with as many presents as we could carry and spent the next hour giving the customary four-kiss goodbye. My longest farewell was spent on the four unopened bottles of champagne that remained in the fridge, bottles that had expected so much more from Party Girl.

❧❧

The next morning, I woke up with a killer headache, stomach ache, and backache. Which didn't come as much surprise since I'd gone to bed with a killer headache, stomach ache, and backache just a few hours earlier.

We ate a quick breakfast at Gilbert's parents' house, then loaded our gifts into the car. More awake than we'd been the previous night, we now had a chance to scope out everyone's gifts.

"Wow, we really got spoiled this year," I said, touched by the thoughtfulness of my welcoming in-laws.

"It's like this every year," Catherine said. "If you can handle sitting at a table for eight hours straight, you're rewarded."

"I'd rather have a four-hour meal and more booze," Gilbert said.

"Or three hours and more champagne," I said, winking at Catherine.

Despite the pains all over my body, I was feeling pretty good. I'd celebrated Christmas far from home—and wouldn't be going back to St. Louis this year—but it still felt like home. My new home.

಄ᔾ

"My stomach is still killing me," I complained to Mika the next day.

"Maybe you just need to fart," Mr. Romance suggested.

"For three days? I don't think so. And my back still hurts, too. The damned headache is finally gone, though."

"Maybe you should go to a doctor?"

French people are always suggesting you go to a doctor. You could have a hangnail and if you said you were going to see the doctor about it they would nod and suggest perhaps you should have gone sooner. But in this case he was right. It was weird that I felt this bad for so long.

I found a doctor down the street and booked an appointment for that evening after work. Having a little time to kill before the appointment, I swung by Starbucks for a holiday latte. I settled into the waiting room, preparing for a long wait, but the doctor called me in nearly as soon as I sat down. I glanced at my latte then back at him. He gave me a look that indicated I could bring the drink in, but that he wasn't happy about it.

I brought it in anyway.

"So, what brings you here today?" he asked.

"My stomach has been bothering me for days, and my lower back too," I answered, then took a sip of my latte.

"Maybe you drink too much coffee?" he suggested.

He could have a point. "Yeah, that's possible. But I figured, hey, my stomach already hurts, so might as well enjoy a holiday latte before they're off the menu!"

He didn't seem to agree with my sound logic. Well, we'll see what you say when the holiday lattes are gone, buddy!

"Hop up here and let's have a look," he said, patting the exam table. "I thought I detected a little accent. Are you English?"

"American."

"American!" he said, switching from French to English. "I love America!"

Then he'd better stop hatin' on my Starbucks!

"How long have you lived here? I love speaking English! Oh this is great. We can speak English during the entire appointment if you like. Or do you prefer French? No, you probably prefer English. Whatever you like!"

I admired his enthusiasm, even though it was making my head spin.

"English would be great. Normally I do try to speak French, but as I'm feeling a little under the weather, English would be easier."

"Under the weather! Ha! I like this expression. But, ah yes, you're here because you're sick. Let's examine you."

He checked my vitals, but seemed more interested in speaking English and talking about America than finding out why I felt like I needed to pass gas 24/7.

"Well, I can't seem to find anything serious. I think

you have what we call a *'crise de foie'*. It's likely you ate too much over the holidays and your body is on overload. I'll write you a prescription for some charcoal pills to help move things along. You can also try to eat healthy and eat less in general for a few days."

He might as well say I should try to turn into a unicorn for a few days. Eat healthy *and* eat less? Nope, not over here.

"And maybe take it easy on the coffee."

Gah, this guy was a buzz kill.

"You can come back anytime! We can speak English! Hope to see you soon!"

Um, dude, you're a doctor. I hope I *don't* see you soon!

ৡৣঌ

"So how did it go?" Mika asked when I returned home.

"I'm having a *crise de foi*."

"A crisis of faith?" he asked, amused.

"What? No, a *crise de foie*. Something to do with my liver. Apparently I ate too much. And I probably need to fart."

"Told you."

The uneasy feeling lasted another week. Sometimes I felt queasy, sometimes it hurt. The charcoal wasn't doing much. I ate healthy and it was the worst. Blech.

Then on the evening of January 5th, I had a revelation. I'd been so focused on my weird stomach pain that I totally forgot we were trying to get pregnant. Could I be...? Could it have happened already?

This wasn't at all what I thought morning sickness would be like. I know everyone says, "Morning? More like all day!" but that's not what I'm talking about. I'm familiar with queasy. I'm old friends with nausea. I've had my fair share of hangovers from my partying days and I've hung my head over a toilet bowl numerous times. I'm no stranger (unfortunately) to vomiting.

This was nothing like that. This was a weird pain that even the doctor couldn't figure out.

Ever the practical one, I restrained myself and didn't take the pregnancy test until the next morning, which is when the instructions said it would be most effective. Pregnancy tests aren't cheap in France and I didn't want to waste one on an ambiguous reading. And while I could hardly sleep that night in anticipation of the morning's Main Event, I wouldn't have been able to sleep if I'd had confusing results either. So we waited until morning.

I took the test.

Before I was even done peeing (because you know I had to peek), two blue lines showed up. Two blue lines. One baby.

When I was done, I slid the test into the convenient pregnancy test holder, which is a brilliant invention that minimizes the grossness of walking around the house displaying a stick you've just peed on.

"So…?" Mika called from the hallway.

I opened the door and held up the stick. "It's not a fart. It's a baby."

"Oh my God."

"I know."

"Oh my God."

"Exciting, huh?"

"Oh my God."

"You can stop saying that now."

"What? Oh yeah, right. I can't believe we're having a baby!"

I thought back to Christmas Eve. I must have been pregnant then. That partially explained the back pain and general discomfort, though I still think the Wooden Stool of Death was mostly responsible for that.

And it explained why I hadn't wanted to drink. But, oh no! I did have a little to drink. Let's see… half a glass of wine and two sips of champagne. It could have been worse. And it's not like I knew it at the time. But Party Girl was gonna have to go on hiatus. Though considering my prolonged *crise de foie* and the fact I'd been working on a fart for several days, drinking would have been off the menu for a long time anyway.

"Monsieur Lesage, are you ready to welcome Baby Lesage into our family?" I asked, wrapping my arms around his waist and leaning back to look up into his big, brown eyes.

"*Oui*, Madame Lesage. I can't think of a better way to start off the new year."

Mock-a-rita

Sometimes, like when you're having a "crisis of faith" or a "liver crisis," you need a non-alcoholic drink but want to partake in the partying. This Mock-a-rita gives you all the flavor, minus the side effects. Warning: Without the influence of alcohol, you might discover your karaoke and/or dancing skills are not as fabulous as you thought!

2 oz. margarita mix (make sure it's the kind without alcohol already in it!)
2 oz. lemon-lime soda
lime
coarse salt

1. Slice the lime in half. Cut one pretty slice for garnish, set the rest aside.
2. Pour margarita mix and soda into a martini shaker filled halfway with ice. Squeeze in some lime juice from the unused portion of lime. Shake lightly.
3. Use the already-squeezed lime to rim your margarita glass, then dip the glass into a plate of salt.
4. Pour the Mock-a-rita mix into your glass (with ice).
5. Garnish with lime slice and enjoy the fact that you'll be hangover-free tomorrow.

Makes 1 serving

11

Sixteen Weeks

By the time I announced my pregnancy to my boss, I had been employed at my French company about a year. I hadn't quite gotten used to the lax French working style and the fact that they only actually work about half the year, once you factor in national holidays, a minimum of five weeks' vacation, and coffee breaks.

So I was shocked to learn I would be getting sixteen weeks of maternity leave. What would I do with all that time? Sure, take care of my baby. But as someone who has worked since age 14, the prospect of four months *sans travail* was hard to imagine.

The typical set-up is six weeks before the due date and ten weeks after. Unlike many American women who work up until their due date (because of an inflexible job or financial concerns or simply wanting to conserve their minimal maternity leave for after the baby arrives), the French really want expecting mothers to take it easy before the birth. And considering France has a lower rate of premature births than the U.S., they're probably right.

According to the official maternity booklet I received at my first prenatal appointment, French health officials have determined that six weeks before the due date is the ideal time to give mama some rest and reduce the risk of a preemie. Any longer is usually unnecessary and any shorter can be risky.

I, of course, didn't heed this advice.

My company's business was seasonal in nature and Christmas was our busiest period. Therefore, no one was allowed to take vacation around the holidays. But I couldn't stomach the thought of spending yet another Christmas apart from my American family.

I ran some numbers. I was due on September 17th, so if I could convince my boss to let me leave only three weeks early instead of six (which is the latest, by law, that you're allowed to work), then I'd have thirteen weeks after the baby was born, meaning I wouldn't come back to work until December 17th—smack dab in the middle of the holiday season. I would probably be allowed to take vacation because, honestly, if they hadn't sorted themselves out by the 17th, they were screwed anyway. Why make me return to work and miss my Christmas if it wouldn't help them?

"Does that sound OK?" I asked my boss, Laurent, and the general manager, Guillaume.

"Christmas is our busiest period. We need you. Take it as a compliment for how much we value you!" Laurent chuckled.

I didn't want a compliment, I wanted to visit my family, you fool.

Guillaume smoothly jumped in before I let a snarky comment slip out. "That sounds reasonable and will allow you time to finish your projects before you leave. But remember, this is an exception to the rule and I expect you to treat it as such."

You mean, next time I'm pregnant I can't go home for Christmas? Deal. We could cross that bridge when we came to it.

"Thank you, Guillaume. I really appreciate it."

ᗕᗏ

The phone rang three times, then went to voice mail. "Hi Mom, it's Vicki," I began.

"Hello?" Doug picked up mid-sentence. Standard practice in my parents' house. Allergic to calls from telemarketers, my mom and step-dad never answer the phone unless they recognize the caller ID. And my French number showed up differently each time for some reason, so they could never be sure it was really me and not someone trying to sell them snake oil. A few times I'd tried to jerk their chain by acting like a telemarketer, but given how often I called, the joke had gotten old pretty quickly. Now I knew to just start talking to the answering machine until they'd vetted my call.

"Hi Doug, how are you?"

"Good, good. Hold on, here's your mom."

"Honey? Hi! Everything OK with the baby?"

Parents always assume the worst.

"Yep, going well. Good news—my Christmas vacation got approved. I only get one week but it's better than nothing."

"Fantastic! We can't wait to see you. Oh, and that reminds me, I booked my ticket to come visit. It's for the last week in September."

"Perfect. Everyone should be out of the hospital by then. So Doug isn't coming?"

"No, he's not up for the trip because of his circulation problems. The long plane ride is going to be a killer."

We chatted a while longer, though it always amazed me we had anything left to say considering we emailed every day and commented on each other's Facebook statuses minutes after they were posted.

"I'd better call Dad. Once he knows you've booked your ticket he'll book his right away. You know how competitive Italians are."

I dialed the Florida number and he picked up on the first ring.

"Well hello! This must be my lovely daughter. To what do I owe this honor?"

He always greeted me that way even though I called every Sunday. But hey, if he thought it was an honor to talk to me I'd go ahead and let him think that.

"Just wanted to say hi. And let you know that Mom booked her ticket for the last week of September. You and Marsha can come any time after that."

Even though they already had quite a few grandchildren, they were still eager to meet their soon-to-be addition.

"OK, so should we book for the first week of October? Will the weather be nice? And can we stay with you in your new apartment?"

Dad always asked questions in threes, making it a race to answer them all before he fired off more.

"The weather will be nice in the beginning of October and we would love it if you stayed with us."

"What airline do you recommend? Should we book today? Do you need us to bring anything?"

"From Orlando I think American might be your best bet but you should check around. Book soon, though. And can you bring some mac and cheese?"

He'd brought twenty boxes of my favorite pasta with artificial cheese flavoring when they'd come for our wedding but those were long gone.

"Sure, no problem. Anything else? You doing OK?

How's Mika?"

I loved talking to him, but Mama needed a nap after all those questions!

Still, I was super excited that my parents were coming to visit. It would help bridge the gap before my regrettably short Christmas vacation.

♀◦♂

"*Oui, bonjour?*" I said, answering a call from an unknown number on my cell phone. I was at work and shouldn't have been taking a personal call, but as it happened so rarely I decided to chance it. It could have been Johnny Depp calling from his vacation home in the south of France, which is totally worth getting in trouble for.

"*Oui, hâllo.* This is probably someone from the hospital but I'm talking super fast so you can't be sure. Now that you're past the five-month mark in your pregnancy, we'd like you to participate in a study with some weird name that you can't understand over the phone. Are you interested? The research from this study can help pregnant women and babies."

"Sure, I would love to help with your mysterious study. What do I need to do?"

"You need to do something—a word you've never heard of—but don't worry, it's non-intrusive."

"OK, sounds like I shouldn't be agreeing to this but I'm going to naively trust you."

"Great! I will mail you more information but as a quick overview, the study will compare the differences in gestational diabetes between women who are of normal weight and women who are obese. We appreciate your time. *Bonne journée!*"

"*Bonne journée,*" I chirped back.

I was happy to assist in their study. As a pregnant

woman, I felt I owed it to society to help out. While pregnancy feels long to the blimped-out woman going through it, it actually only offers a brief window for researchers to conduct studies.

The geeky scientist in me was thrilled to take part. If I understood correctly, I just needed to share the results of my gestational diabetes test (which I had to take anyway) and then they could analyze them against the results of other women, comparing mine to those of obese women.

Wait a minute... I wasn't in the *obese* category, was I? In the U.S. I would be considered normal and my weight gain was on par for my pregnancy, though admittedly it touched the upper limits of acceptability.[2]

But thinking back on all the foxy French ladies in the waiting room at my prenatal appointments, I had a sinking feeling I'd been placed in the overweight category.

Oh well, too late now. I'd already agreed to the study. I suppose all data points are useful, even the chubby data points.

഻ഄ

At my six-month check-up, the doctor from the study stopped in for a quick chat and confirmed I was in the normal group. Yay me! That merited a reward. Perhaps a croissant?

---

[2] Completely unfairly, pregnant women in France are expected to gain roughly 20-27 pounds (9-12 kilos), while in the U.S. the norm is 25-35 pounds (roughly 11-16 kilos). Worse, when I Googled this information, I started to type *prendre kilos pendant grossesse* (gain weight during pregnancy) and it "completed" my search phrase by changing it to *perdre kilos pendant grossesse* (lose weight during pregnancy). They don't even want you indulging in research about weight gain!

Once the doctor left, the *sage-femme* (the prettier-sounding French word for "midwife") proceeded with our appointment. Business as usual—fill out ridiculous amounts of paperwork in an ever-growing dossier (they should weigh *that* at each visit!) and endure a ridiculous lack of privacy in a room with no changing curtain, no paper sheet. Just me, the *sage-femme*, and the breeze blowing on my bare backside.

The one disconcerting piece of information was that my baby's head was already down in birthing position.

"It's not alarming for his head to be down this early but we need to keep an eye on it. And you need to limit your physical activity. Can you run me through a typical day for you?"

Piece of cake. I'd read in my pregnancy books that you shouldn't start any new exercise routine during pregnancy and that you should always stop if it hurts or you get too tired. I knew I wasn't overdoing it.

"Sure! In the morning I do some calisthenics while getting ready, like squats and leg lifts while brushing my teeth and doing my make-up."

Her eyes widened but she let me continue.

"Then it's a 10-minute walk to the Métro, a 35-minute ride where I sometimes find a seat, then a 15-minute walk from the Métro to my office. Oh, and I usually take the stairs when exiting the station because the escalator is always backed up."

She looked about two seconds away from a heart attack but she kept scribbling in my dossier.

"After work, I meet my husband near his office and we walk home, which takes about an hour. So, as you can see, it's only a bit of walking and some calisthenics."

She set her pen down. "OK, here's how it's gonna be from now on. No calisthenics. You can walk to and from the Métro, but you need to find a seat while riding. As a pregnant woman you have the right to a seat so you just have to ask. And no more stairs, understood? You need to severely limit your exercise or the baby could come early and we don't want that."

I nodded, grimly envisioning all the pounds I would pack on with my reduced exercise regimen.

"If you don't listen to me, I will have to stop you from work early," she gently reprimanded.

"No! I can't stop work early! I need to continue as late as possible so I can spend Christmas with my family."

"Then keep that in mind the next time you're too shy to ask for a seat on the Métro or want to take a flight of stairs."

ৡৣ

"How did your appointment go?" Mika asked that night on our walk home from work.

"Fine. I'm in the normal group for the study."

"Ha, I'm sure you're relieved."

"Yeah. But the *sage-femme* said the baby's head is down low and I need to take it easy. I'm sure she's overreacting. You know how the French are, no offense."

"None taken, but maybe you should listen to her?"

"I did! I sat on the Métro and took the escalator instead of the stairs. She said walking is OK." Probably not for an hour but c'mon! I was a naturally active person and was having a hard enough time cutting out the activities she'd said to.

"OK, as long as you're sure," he said, draping an arm around my shoulders.

"I'm sure."

ৡৣ

I shouldn't have been so sure. In focusing on getting the time to spend with my family at Christmas, I hadn't been focusing on keeping my own little family safe. I had thought the *sage-femme* was being a typical French worrywart. I hadn't taken her advice to heart.

My sweet baby Leo was born prematurely, and had to stay in the NICU for 11 days. I blab about this at length in one of my other books so I'll stick to the highlights here. (My dad would say "it's an honor" to read that much and my mom can "never get enough of those babies" but unless you're my mom or my dad—Hi guys!—you'd probably rather I stick to how this relates to Christmas.) We had to endure a tough stay in the hospital, full of worry and regret, but we were some of the lucky ones who got to take a healthy baby home in a relatively short amount of time.

All's well that ends well, right? I suppose so. We'll never really know why Leo was born early, and maybe it would have happened no matter what I did. I had slowed down near the end of my pregnancy but living in Paris involves lots of unavoidable walking and stairs. I gave up worrying about my weight, because the gestational diabetes tests indicated I was doing just fine (clearly they weren't studying my bloated face), but I couldn't resist a pastry here and there. I tried to eat healthy, I tried to follow doctors' orders, I tried to stay cool in the un-air-conditioned summer heat. I tried to do everything right but it was all so much.

We chose to focus on the bright side: a beautiful baby boy who got to meet his American grandparents at Christmas time. Of course, that trip was a whole other story...

Skinny French Martini

It's hard to be a normal-sized woman among a sea of stick-thin French women. It's even harder when you're a pregnant bloated whale. This is the perfect post-pregnancy cocktail: heavy on alcohol, light(er) on calories. Vive La France, I can fit into my pants!

1 1/2 oz. vodka
1/2 oz. Chambord
3 oz. light pineapple juice
1 twist lemon peel

1. Pour vodka, Chambord, and pineapple juice into a martini shaker filled with ice. Shake well.
2. Strain into a martini glass, drop in the lemon peel, and enjoy your non-expanding waistline!

Makes 1 serving

12

Foie Gras and Egg Snot

Snap! I secured the lid on my ginormous Tupperware container and patted the top. "There, all set! You think they'll like it?" I asked Mika as he was getting ready for work.

"They'll love it," he replied. Though as a winner of the Most Supportive Husband of the Year Award, he wasn't exactly objective.

I'd slaved over my pasta salad the previous night in preparation for my company's Christmas potluck lunch. The office busybody had informed me I could bring anything I liked, it just had to be Christmas-themed.

So I cooked up a boatload of fusilli and tossed it with diced red and green peppers and a homemade (thank you, Mika) vinaigrette. I topped it off with a snow-dusting of Parmesan. Perfect amount of holiday cheer. My co-workers would devour it!

A few minutes before the party was scheduled to

start, I transferred my pasta salad to a serving bowl. An enormous Titanic of a bowl. Man. I'd really gone overboard. But I had 40 people to feed! This stuff would surely go like hotcakes.

My colleagues trickled in to the lunchroom and started setting up their offerings. They laid out *foie gras* with mini toasts, assorted cheeses and hand-sliced sausages, fresh baguettes, and fresh fruit. Everything looked *très* appetizing.

"This isn't very Christmassy," the office busybody said, eyeing my mountain of pasta salad. "Who brought this?" Nothing like potluck-shaming your co-workers to get them in the holiday spirit.

"Um, that's mine," I said more sheepishly than I should have. Considering I usually microwaved my meals or got takeout, I was quite proud of my creation.

"Is this... traditional Christmas food in the U.S.?" she asked, as if she was trying to give me an out. Like, if I would admit that this grotesque concoction of pasta and cheese and vegetables was foreign, then she'd be able to sell it to everyone else.

"Not really. But it's red and green! With snow! Like Christmas!"

"Oh, I get it, I guess. It's *abstract*." She said the word as if she'd smelled a fart. Then she passed over my dish and served herself a hunk of *foie gras*.

I kept an eye on my Jackson Pollock pasta salad as the party kicked into gear, but I had no takers. Maybe they were afraid to mess up the pristine snow-capped mountain? I eased over and scooped a mound onto my plate. There. Now it wasn't so intimidating. And if people saw that someone else had taken the plunge, they might dive in as well.

Nope, nothing. People piled their plates higher and higher with *saucisson* and Camembert, but no one wanted my expressionist fusilli.

I enlisted help from my buddy Theo, who would eat anything. When we went out for pizza, he made sure nothing was left on anyone's plate. If someone couldn't finish a slice, he'd gladly scoop it up. Bite taken out of it? No problem. Bits and scraps with sauces and unidentified blobs splattered on them? While I was busy gagging at the thought, he'd down whatever remained. This was my guy.

"Hey, Theo. Can you do me a solid?"

"What?" His English was good but admittedly that was an odd expression. In fact, I'd never even used it before in my life so I have no idea why I chose to use it then.

"Um, could you please do me a favor?"

"Sure!" You gotta love someone who blindly agrees to a favor, especially when they just thought it involved something about a solid.

"Can you scoop some of that pasta salad on to your plate? Maybe walk around eating it so people see it's not radioactive or poisonous?"

"It's not radioactive or poisonous, right?"

"Probably not."

"Good enough for me."

He obliged and heaped a gargantuan pile of pasta salad on his plate, though it hardly left a dent in my Mountain of Embarrassment. He took it one step further and cruised around the room proclaiming, "Mmmm, this pasta salad is the best I've *ever* had!"

His positive endorsement didn't lead to any takers. Undoubtedly because they knew he'd eat anything.

Just then, Eddy, our normally antisocial colleague, burst into the kitchen with a stack of four pizza boxes and a huge smile on his face. Everyone's eyes followed the boxes until he set them down on the buffet table and opened them one by one.

No one was more excited about the pizza than me. I

love me some *foie gras*, but pizza? That's where my cholesterol-filled heart lies.

But why were my colleagues so excited? Minutes ago they were shunning my pasta salad for its non-adherence to traditional Christmas fare but now they were drooling over chain-store pizza? And treating Eddy the Jerk like some kind of hero, as if whipping out a credit card was anywhere near as hard as cooking four tons of pasta. Not fair! When my mom had told me as a kid that life wasn't fair, this was not the scene I envisioned. I expected to have to fight for equal pay for equal work, and to fight my brother for the last scoop of ice cream. I did not expect my homemade pasta salad to be upstaged by some stupid store-bought pizza pies.

But if you can't beat 'em, eat all their pizza. I headed over to see what all the fuss was about. To see which mouthwatering flavors awaited me…

I should have known better. This is France, Home of Super Weird Pizza Toppings.

Pizza #1: Ground Beef and Potatoes

I have no problem with ground beef, but potatoes? For a nation that thrives on leafy salads and small portions, this hearty pizza seems incredibly out of place. And while I'm a big fan of carbs, I don't need pizza crust *and* potatoes. That's like putting crackers on a sandwich or cookies on your donuts. (Hold on, did someone say donuts?) The ingredients are fine separately but we don't need to be beaten over the head with them.

Pizza #2: Smoked Salmon and Crème Fraiche

What the what? Fish has no place on a pizza. I learned this lesson the hard way during the summer I lived in Seattle. The Pacific Northwest is known for their salmon and it is divine. My Italian godfather and his Thai wife, who I lived with, loaded me up with noodle-heavy meals every night. So I opted for salmon wherever I could. And then one day I took it too far.

"I like pizza. I like salmon. Why not have salmon pizza?"

Here's why not: because it smells like rotten garbage. The salmon flavor takes over all the other flavors, making the cheese taste like fish, the sauce taste like fish, and the crust taste like—you guessed it—fishy fish that smells like fish. But the worst part is that the salmon *doesn't* taste like fish! It tastes like garbage-flavored cheese and garbage-flavored sauce. Like Jennifer Aniston and Vince Vaughan, salmon and pizza are each wonderful and amazing on their own, but are a total disaster together.

France's take on salmon pizza is even worse because it's smoked salmon, which is even more pungent. And while crème fraiche is a ritzier cousin to sour cream, it's still cream. On a pizza. And not even spread out smoothly, oh no. You'll get three randomly spaced globs of the gunk, with smoked salmon swimming in between. No, *merci*.

Pizza #3: Egg and Sausage

Are we eating breakfast? I'm actually a huge fan of pizza for breakfast, especially back in my partying days when many a morning was met with a vicious hangover that only inordinate amounts of grease could tame. But (and you might be noticing a trend here), I don't want breakfast on my pizza. Much like the beef and potatoes concoction, I have no problem with the sausage part of this equation, but that egg came straight out of left field.

Let's take a quick multiple choice quiz:

Question: If you encounter an egg on a French pizza,

how is this egg likely to be cooked?

Answer: Choose one of the following responses, if you can suppress your gag reflex long enough to read them all.

A. Scrambled, which is strange but perhaps the most innocuous way to put egg on a pizza.

B. Hard-boiled, which would bestow a strong sulphur flavor on the pizza but would at least have a palatable consistency.

C. Poached, which would be a daring move because once you pop it, runny yolk goo would flood your pizza.

D. Just-barely-fried, which would resemble a pool of uncooked snot right in the middle of your pizza, making you realize that options A through C were not nearly as disgusting as you'd originally thought.

The answer is three helpings of D. That's right, not one snotty booger ball but three!

Pizza #4: Pepperoni and Peppers

Now, what could I possibly have to say about this pizza? Sounds perfect, right? That's because it is! And clearly my colleagues agreed because they devoured it all before I could even snag one slice. That would be annoying enough because, hello, pizza.

But I have an even bigger problem with this. Do you notice something about this fourth pizza? The one that has cheese, carbs, and red and green peppers? Does it sound a little bit like THE EXACT SAME INGREDIENTS AS MY PASTA SALAD? Oh, so *now* we like peppers and cheese! *Now* we don't care if it's traditional Christmas food or not. *Now* we're suddenly into abstract expressionism with a palette of red and green peppers tossed haphazardly onto a doughy canvas.

As I watched everyone masticating their slices, leaving me and my shameful pasta salad on the sidelines, I grew more and more pissed off. Other than Theo, everyone had made me feel awkward. That wasn't the Christmas spirit was it? I was surrounded by a room full of grinches. Pasta-salad-hating grinches. I was going to get back at—

POP!

Our boss's father had popped open the champagne, and was pouring the overflowing bottle into a glass.

"Here, Vicki," he said. "You get the first glass. I know how much you like champagne."

What had I been saying? I think something along the lines of, "I love my co-workers." I downed that first glass and my boss's father promptly poured another. I served myself some *foie gras* and Camembert, and tore off a hunk of fresh baguette. This party was actually quite awesome.

That, and champagne has a powerful effect on me. Cheers!

Irish Cream Egg Nog

As you might have picked up on by now, I like eggs but I don't like preparing them. The runny, icky consistency really gets to me. So this recipe bypasses the egg-preparing part and gets straight to the good part: the cocktail. If you prefer to make your own egg nog, be my guest! And, um, can I be *your* guest? I do like me some homemade egg nog.

2 oz. Irish cream liqueur
3 oz. store-bought egg nog
whipped cream

1. Pour the Irish cream and egg nog into a martini shaker filled with ice.
2. Give it two good shakes, then strain into a tumbler glass.
3. Top with whipped cream (squeezing a little in your mouth while you're at it because, hello, whipped cream) and toast to one of the best uses of eggs around.

Makes 1 serving

13

Warning: May Contain Fingers

Still trembling from the infamous Jackson Pollock Pasta Salad Disaster the previous year, I was nervous about what to bring to this year's office potluck. I was pregnant with Baby #2 and perpetually exhausted from chasing my toddler around, so I was in no mood to make something fancy. Especially not something that would get rejected anyway.

Fortunately I found my out. "We're doing a joint Christmas party and going away party for Brigitte," the office busybody informed me. "So don't forget to bring something special!"

Are potato chips and hummus special enough? Because that's what you're getting, lady!

Being in the "I eat everything I see" stage of my pregnancy (that stage lasts about nine months), I showed up early to the party. My co-workers have this annoying habit of not letting anyone nibble until it's all prepared. I have this annoying habit of not caring and eating anyway. Sorry, but a potluck for 40 people takes way too long to set up. You think I can resist dipping potato chips into hummus? Show me the person who can. SHOW ME.

My friend Fanny popped in with homemade pizza squares and asked me to heat them up while she finished something for work. No problem! If by "heat them up" she meant "eat them up" (see what I did there?).

A nanosecond after the microwave dinged, I shoved a pizza slice in my mouth and carried the rest over to the couch, where I parked my ever-growing butt and dug in.

"*Attention, il y a un doigt dedans!*" My co-worker Camille's warning—"Watch out, there's a finger in there!"—made no sense. I shrugged off her comment and continued stuffing my face.

What had she meant "there's a finger in there"? Was it a French expression? I often misunderstood those. Or maybe it's like if you only want a little whiskey you say "just a finger." So maybe she meant there weren't that many pizza slices? As in, there wouldn't be enough for me? Oh, maybe she meant not to eat them all because there weren't that many *and* other people might want to eat them. I guess that was it. Still, a roundabout way to say it.

And also, way too late, honey. I'd already made it more than halfway through the Tupperware container before I'd worked out what I thought she meant.

Colleagues trickled into the lunchroom as I avoided their gaze. I should have been embarrassed about how much pizza I'd hogged but I was more afraid they would take it away from me.

"Where's my pizza?" Fanny asked.

Busted. "Over here, Fanny!" I said, licking my fingers after polishing off the last slice. "Sorry, I couldn't help myself."

"Ha, no problem. Glad they were so tasty! So, did

you find my finger in there?"

"What's this everyone's saying about a finger? There wasn't *actually* a finger in there, was there?" I looked down at the empty container and my pregnant belly. Was a severed digit floating around in there?

Fanny stuck out a bandaged finger. Oh my God. I felt the bile rise in my throat.

"I cut it last night making the pizzas. A big piece came off, actually. Don't worry," she quickly added, noting my horrified expression. "It happened while I was chopping a pepper to put on top. I don't think the finger got in with the pizza slices. At least, I hope not. I brushed all the peppers in the trash without looking."

"Are you OK? And, more importantly, how could you not look?" I would be way too curious to see what a no-longer-connected bit of my finger looked like to just brush it in the trash without a backward glance.

"Oh yeah, I'm fine."

"Can I see your finger?" I was concerned for my friend but I also had to see how much of her finger was missing. It couldn't be too bad if she hadn't gone to the hospital.

"Sure," she said, pulling the bandage off.

The amount missing was just enough to make me lose my appetite. I tried not to show it, for fear of alerting her to the fact that she now only had 9 and 7/8ths fingers. "That doesn't look too bad. I'm sure it will heal in no time." Yeah right! There was like a quarter of an inch missing! Which meant a quarter of an inch of finger was possibly cart-wheeling around my tummy.

On the bright side, at least there's a lot of protein in it.

And at least this Christmas, someone's dish was attracting more negative attention than mine!

Whiskey Nog

Here's another egg nog recipe, once again made with store bought nog because it's not like I've gotten over my egg phobia since the last chapter.

1 oz. whiskey (also known as a "finger" of whiskey)
4 oz. store-bought egg nog
dash of vanilla syrup
nutmeg for garnish

1. Pour the whiskey and egg nog into a martini shaker filled with ice. Add a dash of vanilla syrup.
2. Give it two good shakes, then strain into the glass of your choice.
3. Dust with nutmeg to make it look fancy. Drink with your pinky out to look even fancier (and to show off the fact that you still have all your fingers).

Makes 1 serving

Have Holiday Cheer, Will Travel

Going on vacation for the holidays, even if it kills us

14

Feliz Navidad

"Mi casa es su casa!"

I'd studied French in high school but I was pretty sure that bit of Spanish meant "My house is your house." Which was weird because we were at a hotel.

My college boyfriend, Mark, and I had just arrived in Badajoz, Spain. We'd be spending Christmas with María Teresa and María José, twin sisters who were friends with Mark's mom. We would later tour other parts of Spain but wanted to be with family—if not our own families then at least *someone's* family—for the holidays.

We'd arrived in the picturesque village on a Sunday, a few days before Christmas. María José picked us up from the train station and drove us to our hotel. "We picked the best one for you. We spared no expense. Money is no object when it comes to guests!"

Fabulous! Except we were the ones paying. She'd graciously booked the hotel (which would have been no easy feat for us considering this small town near the Portuguese border boasted few English speakers). But it was still my credit card on the line so I felt her generosity was a little unwarranted. Not that I expected her to pay for our hotel. Just that she wouldn't take credit for it.

"Here are your keys. I checked in for you earlier so the desk clerk could go home." That was nice. Maybe I shouldn't have been so harsh. "I let you settle in. We come pick you up tomorrow morning. *Buenas noches!*"

Mmm, nachos.

"I'm starving," Mark and I said at the same time. We'd left Madrid that morning and taken a series of trains across the country to arrive at our destination, with nothing more than a *jamón* sandwich to tide us over.

"Where do you think we can get food around here?" he asked me, as if I had any idea. "On the ride over it looked like everything was closed."

Never one to stop thinking about food, I had already realized the same thing. The austere hotel didn't have a restaurant. And since the front desk clerk had already left for the night, we had no one to ask.

"Let's drop off our suitcases, then have a look around," I suggested.

The typically European hotel room was smaller than my dorm room back at college. But it was tidy and cute and would serve its purpose.

"Shall we?" I asked Mark, my stomach audibly growling.

We ventured out into the silent night. Not a single light flickered in the windows of the neighboring buildings. No neon signs indicating available grub. I had dreamed of *tapas* and *rioja* and *croquetas*. I'd settle for a bag of chips and a soda.

As we headed up to the main road, figuring we'd have more luck there, a scooter whizzed past.

"Did you see that?" I asked. "It looked like a pizza

delivery guy!"

We looked at each other and grinned. "Chase that scooter!"

Of course, by the time we reached the main road the scooter was out of sight.

"If he was heading out for a delivery," Mark said, "then the pizza shop must be the other direction. In which case, we just have to wait for him to come back and then follow him. But if he was on his way *back* from a delivery, we should head the direction he was going."

"Logical, Mr. Engineering Major," I said. "But it still doesn't help. We've got a 50/50 chance of picking the right direction."

"True. But if we follow him, we could find the store. Worst case, we'll meet up with him sooner, maybe even stop him and ask where the store is."

"Good point." We headed in the direction the scooter had whizzed past. We walked for 15 minutes without hearing the telltale whir of the scooter's engine.

"Shouldn't we have run into him by now? This town isn't *that* big."

Mark didn't say anything but his stomach roared in reply.

All of a sudden, the scooter turned a corner and zipped past us. We hopped around, flailing our arms, trying to flag him down. He either didn't see us or wanted to stay far away from the crazy Americans jumping in the street. We chased after him but lost him down a side street.

"How many side streets does this town have?"

Again Mark didn't reply. His extreme hunger had turned into extreme grumpiness.

We wandered around the deserted town for another 30 minutes, me thinking I would never eat again, Mark only looking straight ahead with determined focus.

"So what do you think the Marías have planned for

us tomorrow?" I asked.

"I don't care, but I hope it involves food."

"WHIZZZZZ." That blasted scooter passed us on another side street.

"I'm still glad we came," I said, "even though we're never going to eat again."

"Need... food..."

"WHIZZZZ." The scooter was just taunting us now.

"I can't wait until tomorrow when we can try real Spanish cuisine."

"Blergh... flargh... food."

We turned a corner, and saw the prettiest, most welcoming sign on the planet: PIZZA.

Bells jingled on the door as Mark opened it and we stepped inside. The smell of cheese and marinara sauce and grease sent us into sensory overload. We reverted to cavemen and simply grunted and pointed to place our order, thus improving Spain's impression of Americans ten-fold.

Once handed our cardboard boxes filled with slices of heaven, we headed outside to eat them on the curb like the classy travelers we are.

We scarfed down the pizza like we hadn't seen food in weeks, or at least a few hours. We picked off the little bits of cheese that had stuck to the cardboard. We licked our greasy fingers clean. We enjoyed that pizza like no pizza has been enjoyed before.

"Tomorrow we'll be more Spanish."

৵৹৻

The next day, María José picked us up as promised, accompanied by her nephew Pedro. They drove us to the neighboring town of Cáceres, known for its winding passages and storks perched on rooftops. The old town is so well-preserved, with very few signs of modern culture, that it's often used to film movies set in medieval times. I was thankful we hadn't been chasing the pizza guy around *these* ancient streets.

Pedro knew everything about Cáceres. "This is the street you see in films. There aren't many people around and it's cheap to set up here. *Treasure Island* and *1492: The Conquest of Paradise* were filmed here." I snapped a photo so I could say I'd walked on a street that was in a movie.

He led us up to a high point in the city where we looked out across a flat plain. "That over there is Portugal."

As in, the country? How could you be standing in one place and see another country? Too cool. I wasn't sure I believed him, but snapped a picture anyway.

"Maybe we need a break?" he asked. "We go to a café."

I nodded emphatically in agreement. I was still scarred from the previous evening's hunger scare.

We found a cozy café and tumbled inside. "I order for you, yes? I pick something special."

Worked for me. I was excited to try something traditionally Spanish, ashamed of my pizza-gorging the night before.

Pedro ordered *treis* of something and then proceeded to share more history about the region. His English was great and I loved his accent. He pronounced his V's like B's, so my name became Bicki.

"Ah Mark and Bicki, here we go!" he said, as the waiter set down three steaming mugs of what looked like melted chocolate.

I dove right in. This was no simple hot chocolate. I'm not even sure it contained milk. It was as if someone had melted a chocolate bar and added a dash of cream.

I wanted to savor it but couldn't help myself. I slurped it up, absorbed in my own world of chocolatey goodness. When I finally came up for air, Pedro and

Mark were staring at me. They hadn't even touched their treats.

Uh oh. I'd definitely done something wrong. I wiped the chocolate mustache from my upper lip.

"Well, Bicki, that's one way to do it," Pedro said. "But now what will you dip your churros in?"

Right then the waiter arrived with a basket of long, thin cinnamon pastries.

Ah, I saw now. That's why the chocolate was so thick—it wasn't meant for drinking, it was meant for dipping. Well, they shouldn't make it so darn delicious if they don't want me to slam the whole thing. And they should serve the churros at the same time if they don't want idiots like me to get confused!

"Whoops," I said, figuring I should admit my faux pas even though I would definitely do it again if someone set a steaming mug of melted chocolate in front of me. "I guess I'll just have to eat my churros plain." As if that was some kind of torture.

Mark had a smug smile on his face, as if he was so superior because he had intuitively known that you shouldn't chug a mug of chocolate just in case there might be churros coming.

"No, no, we get you another mug!" Pedro insisted. He motioned for the waiter to come over and pointed at my empty mug. The waiter understood immediately. I must not have been the first customer to drink the dipping sauce.

Moments later, the waiter set a fresh cup of steaming chocolate in front of me. I gave Mark a smug little smile of my own. One that said, "I may be clueless when it comes to foreign customs, but I'm the one who got two mugs of chocolate." I snapped a photo of that, too.

৵৵

Still not fully immersed in Spanish cuisine, I was determined to give it an honest go before we left the country.

Pedro picked us up on Christmas Eve morning (Is there another name for that? Seems like there should be a less confusing way to say that.) and took us on a tour of Badajoz. We stopped in for chocolate and churros here, espresso there. A little sightseeing *aquí*, a little Spanish history *allá*.

When afternoon hit, we commenced a five-hour bar crawl that included as much tapas and sangria as you could feast your eyes on. We met Pedro's friends. We spoke to strangers. The more sangria I drank, the more fluent in Spanish (I thought) I became.

"*Gracias*, Pedro. This day has been awesome."

"*De nada*, Bicki."

When night fell, we headed to María Teresa's house for the festivities.

More tapas.

More sangria.

A martini glass full of shrimp cocktail, with a sauce that tasted curiously like Big Mac sauce, but I didn't dare vocalize my impression.

A traditional Portuguese Christmas Eve dish of *bacalhau* (salted cod) with potatoes.

Country cured *jamón* so fresh off the bone that it was literally carved off the leg in front of me. That admittedly took some getting used to.

"Come into our dining room, where the walls are hung with expensive art, and the side table boasts a wooden pig leg stand, with a pig leg standing in it."

Of course María Teresa didn't say this. And of course she didn't need to because when I entered the dining room I saw the Giant Pig Leg Stand® for myself.

Now, I'm the furthest thing from a vegetarian. I like me some meat. Steak? I'm all over it. Pork chops? Sure, why not? Duck, quail, even rabbit? Hey, I've lived in France for 10 years. You can't scare me! Hot dogs? I don't need to know what part of the pig they come from (no, seriously, I don't, so please don't ruin the illusion for me). Just slather on some ketchup and mustard and call it a day.

So, yes, I eat meat. But… only when I can pretend it might not have come from an animal. Steak? Grows on trees. Pork chops? Aren't those a root vegetable? Duck, quail, rabbit? I think they ripen on the vine. Hot dogs? I TOLD YOU NOT TO TELL ME WHERE THEY COME FROM!

In France, when you order fish an actual fish will be sitting on your plate. Like, with its head and eyes and tail and all its fishy bits. I thought fish came breaded in little boxes? I also thought we agreed not to shatter the illusion!

So imagine how I felt when the slab of dried meat formerly known as a pig's leg was sitting on a display stand manufactured for this very purpose. As in, many people do this and think it's totally normal.

"Bicki, more *jamón*?" Pedro asked, hovering over the pig leg and brandishing a sharp knife.

"*Sí, por favor.*" What can I say? I wanted to be polite. And that was some damn tasty ham. As long as I didn't see where it was coming from.

After Pedro and the Marías stuffed us full of delectable farm-grown food, we headed into the study (The study! As if we were in Clue! "It was Bicki, in the study, with a wooden pig leg stand.") for after-dinner drinks and gift-opening.

Pedro poured everyone a glass of port wine, another "traditional" custom since they lived so close to the Portuguese border. He raised his glass to toast, then stopped himself. "Wait! We forgot the most important tradition!"

He rushed out of the room and rummaged in the hall closet. He returned holding something behind his back.

What could it be? A crown of candles, like they wear in Sweden? A wooden shoe, like they have in Holland?

"Reindeer antlers!" he said with a level of pride heretofore unseen whilst giving someone a headband with fabric reindeer antlers shooting out the top. "Here, put them on!"

I happily obliged, thrilled that while we could be drinking port wine in a glamorous Spanish study, we could also wear cheesy reindeer antlers to get in the holiday spirit.

I may think their shrimp cocktail sauce tastes like Big Mac sauce. I unceremoniously flail my arms to flag down pizza delivery guys on scooters. I may wrinkle my nose at giant ham legs on display. But somehow, in the middle of this small Spanish village, this gauche American managed to fit right in.

Badajoz Sangria

Since Badajoz, Spain is so close to the Portuguese border, many of their dishes (and drinks) are inspired by their neighbor to the west. I love sangria and I love port wine, so this recipe is a festive combination of both!

1/4 cup water
1/3 cup sugar
1 bottle red wine
12 oz. port wine
1 pineapple, cut into chunks
2 oranges, cut into chunks
2 limes, cut into chunks

1. Pour water into a large pitcher. Add sugar and stir.
2. Add red wine, port wine, and fruit chunks.
3. If possible, chill before serving (even overnight).
4. To serve, pour over a glass of ice. Reindeer antlers optional.

Makes 8 servings

15

Wheezing the Juice

Encino Man changed my life in three profound ways:

1. I fell in love with Brendan Fraser. Even though now I don't think he's quite as hunky as my 12-year-old self thought, there will always be a sacred corner of my heart that beats for this man.
2. I will always think Pauly Shore is hilarious. Which means I've drastically limited the number of people willing to be my friend. And I'm OK with that because while you're over there saying he doesn't have a funny bone in his body I'll be over here wheezing the juice.
3. It instilled in me a strong desire to visit Estonia.

So for the winter holidays of 2007, I did just that. My boyfriend at the time, Pierre, and I headed to Tallinn for a long weekend.

We booked a luxurious hotel that was suspiciously cheap. It was a bit of a walk from the Old Town, but it was worth it to be staying at what was supposedly a spa resort.

I'd envisioned Nordic steam rooms, Swedish massages, and luxuriant manicures and pedicures.

I should have realized the former Soviet Union was a little further away from Scandinavia.

My first spa treatment was a massage with Helga. I waited in the brightly lit waiting room, lined with bland folding chairs, hoping the massage room itself would feel less industrial.

"Wicki?" A burly woman nearly twice my height and twice my width with a coin-sized mole on her cheek opened the door to the waiting room. At this point I was used to anyone from a country east of France calling me Wicki instead of Vicki.

"Yes," I said, almost as a question, not sure I wanted to admit I was Wicki, in fear of what this giantess had planned for me.

"You come."

Yes, ma'am! I followed her down an equally bright, equally industrial hallway and into the massage room.

It was stark as could be. Blinding lights, gleaming white cabinets, and a pleather massage contraption in the middle. Not quite a chair, not quite a table.

"I'm Helga. You take off clothes. I do massage." She and her mole stared at me.

Now, I'm no prude. I mean that literally—*now* I'm no prude. I've been to the Blue Lagoon in Iceland, where you have to shower naked before hopping in the warm springs. I've given birth to two French-American children without so much as a paper blanket between my business and the 42-person staff that examined me throughout my pregnancies. But that is now, this was then.

Back then I could count on one hand the number of people who'd seen me naked. Helga and her mole were about to be added to that list.

I stripped down in front of her, mercifully allowed to keep my underwear on, and approached the medieval cushioned device. She guided me in with strong expert hands.

"You relax. I massage."

"OK—" I started, then she karate-chopped my back, knocking the wind out of me. Maybe I'd skip the talking. She and her mole didn't seem the chatty types anyway.

Helga pounded on my back like she hated it. She kneaded my muscles in every direction. She worked muscles I didn't even know I had.

I closed my eyes. WHACK! Helga struck my back.

I sought out peace and zen. WHOOMP. A thump on my butt.

I pictured running in a field. BLA-BLOOMP. She slammed my thighs together.

If she was preparing me for a barbecue, I'd have made for a very tender slab of meat.

THWACK! She flipped me over and began "massaging" (if we were still calling it that) my front.

I didn't know how much more of this I could take. She was beating the hell out of me. I half-expected the fluorescent lights to show bruises all over my body, but when I finally lifted my lids I saw I was fine. And believe it or not, I felt... good.

"You like? We finish. We can do again tomorrow. You must book appointment, though. I'm wery busy."

She had people lining up for this? I guess I could kind of see why. I hobbled out of there, feeling light as a feather. A feather that had just had the crap beat out of it.

೦∾ଓ

"I'm getting a manicure before we go out tonight," I said to Pierre. I slipped a pair of gold earrings on as the finishing touch for my sparkly New Year's Eve outfit.

"Sounds good. I'll meet you in the lobby."

"Cool. Give me about 45 minutes?"

I headed to the hotel's nail salon, and was met with, of course, a brightly lit industrial room.

Nadia, the manicurist I'd booked with, was waiting for me.

"We go," she said in a tone that seemed way too gruff for her petite frame.

I couldn't expect her to be thrilled at having to do someone's nails when she'd rather be getting her New Year's Eve groove on, but it's not my fault she had to work. I'd give her a big tip to help make up for it.

"Pick color," she said, pointing to a display of 42 shades of trashy pink and red nail polishes. I had a hard time selecting an understated hue amongst options like Hot Pink Hooker, Prostitute Plum, and Lady of the Midnight Blue. I selected the palest pink I could find, but it was still about as subtle as a drag queen in a disco.

"Good choice. We begin?"

She yanked my hand across the table and started scraping and cutting. Bits of skin and cuticle flew about the room. Was she related to Helga?

I couldn't bear to look, afraid of what I'd find. I went back to my zen-seeking, field-running fantasy, hoping to tune out under the blazing lights.

"There. We finish."

I held up my hands, examining my nails. Fierce pink surrounded by red bloody scabs.

"Thank you," I said, as I gave her a generous tip and got the hell out of there. Thank you for making me look like a hooker who just got out of a fight. A fight that I must have won, though, or else my nails would be in much worse shape.

"Hey!" Pierre said, linking his arm in mine as we headed out for the evening. "How was your manicure?"

"Spectacular," I said, holding up a hand for him to see.

"*Merda*, what the hell happened? You look like a p-r-o-s-"

"Prostitute that got in a fight. I know. Shall we?"

As we stepped out into the cold Estonian air, this lady of the night was ready for a night on the town.

࿓ঔৎ

"The menu is in Russian. How am I supposed to order?" Pierre asked me.

"As opposed to Estonian?" I retorted. "You would have been able to order in Estonian?"

"Touché."

We had settled on a touristy medieval-themed Russian restaurant for dinner. We figured we should eat up before partying for the New Year and not many other places were open.

Our waitress arrived and set a tray in front of us: two shots and a bowl of pickles. "You start with this, then I take your order."

"Thank you," I said with a smile. "Oh, and could we please get a menu in English?" After Helga and Nadia, I was growing fearful of Estonian women, but I had to ask.

"No. All the other tables using them."

Might as well take those shots, then. "*Na Zdorovie!*" we said in unison as we each slammed our shot and chased it with a pickle.

Our waitress came back with more shots. "Ready to order? We all out of bear. But everything else on menu is available."

There was *bear* on the menu?

We took turns pointing to the menu, not having any idea what we were ordering, only knowing that it wasn't bear.

"*Na Zdorovie!*" we said again, slamming our shots. Well, no matter what we ended up ordering, at least I had two pickles to tide me over.

❧

After finishing my mystery meal—I think it was some sort of game hen—I headed to the restroom. They had taken the medieval theme to a serious extreme. No overhead lights, just candles. The toilets flushed for real, but to wash your hands, you had to turn a crank that spilled a series of buckets into the sink. Then to dry your hands, you tugged a paper towel from a stack that was still in its jumbo pack wrapping. You know, just like in the middle ages.

We stepped out of the restaurant, past a fake bear holding the menu, as giant snowflakes started falling to the cobblestoned street. The scene was enchanting. The beauty of the snow against the crumbling buildings, juxtaposed against the tackiness of the bear and my manicure. Somehow it was perfect.

Also, I was drunk off vodka.

I didn't know where the night would take us. Or the New Year. I didn't know what my future held. How long I would stay with Pierre. How long I would stay in France.

All I knew was that it didn't matter. Right there, in that moment, I had found zen. Transported back in time, not quite to the Stone Age of *Encino Man*, but to the middle ages of Estonia, we wandered the ancient streets of Tallinn in search of a modern-day nightclub, knowing that wherever we ended up would be a memorable experience.

And with any luck, we could swing by a Quikee Mart on the way home and wheeze some juice.

The Juice Wheezer

If you're looking to slurp down some juice, this cocktail is for you. Loaded with three different juices, it tastes so good you'll hardly notice the alcohol. Which means you'd better not slurp too much, or the alcohol is going to sneak up on you!

1 oz. vodka
1 oz. coconut rum
1 oz. pineapple juice
1 oz. orange juice
1 oz. cranberry juice

1. Combine all ingredients in a martini shaker with ice.
2. Shake, then pour into a glass of your choice (or directly in your mouth if you really want to stay true to the "wheezing the juice" theme. Not responsible for any resulting messes.)

Makes 1 serving

16

U.S. Bound

International flights are never easy, but with a 17-month-old they are a true test of your patience. I didn't need a test because I already knew my results: I had zero patience.

Granted post-holiday vacation from work, we were headed to St. Louis to visit my family for two weeks in January. Mom and Doug promised to keep the Christmas decorations up, and Dad and Marsha were flying up from Florida. We would get to see everyone, if only we could get there.

Fortunately, our curious little boy actually behaved himself during the 9 1/2 hour flight to Chicago. He found an empty cabinet near our seat (thank you, plane interior designers!) and contented himself with opening it, smiling at us, closing it, smiling at us, and repeating for three hours.

At one point, a passenger ran past him, threw up on

the floor, and then fainted. This provided an additional hour of interest for Leo, and even though I knew I should give the man some privacy, I thought it would be better for everyone on the plane if my son was occupied, albeit by gawking at a stranger's misfortune.

Also, as someone who had thrown up on a plane before, I was curious to see it from the other perspective. Hey, it's a long flight. How else are you going to pass the time?

"Welcome to Chicago, where the temperature is -11 degrees. We touched down on time, but we'll be waiting on the tarmac for a few minutes due to the weather."

No problem, I could handle a few minutes. The trip had gone surprisingly smoothly up to that point, with no crying (from me or Leo) and now here we were on time!

Two hours later, we were still waiting on the tarmac. The brutally low temperatures meant the airport employees could only be outside for five-minute intervals, thus causing a monumental backup in directing planes to their gates, setting up jet bridges, and unloading luggage.

Our fellow passengers panicked at the delay, but I was cool as a cucumber. "Don't worry, Mika. There are connecting flights from Chicago to St. Louis every hour so even if we miss ours, we can catch the next one. Worst case, we can always drive." I laughed. "Though I'd be surprised if it came to that."

Once we were set free, passengers clawed over each other to escape. The mass of humanity headed up the jetway, where a somber-faced gate agent directed us to a wall pinned with tickets for rebooked flights. I doubted ours would be up there but checked anyway.

ST. LOUIS-LESAGE screamed at me beneath a skull-and-crossbones sketched on the front of the envelope.

Why were *we* being rebooked? Hopefully it was for

the next flight.

I opened the envelope to discover that we'd been rebooked for two days later.

"Mika, this is outrageous! We're rebooked for Wednesday!"

Mika's face fell while Leo glanced around for some trouble to cause. "I'm not staying in freezing ass Chicago for two days. I want to visit your family!"

"Screw this. We're driving. It's only five hours."

But before we could leave we had to go through passport control, retrieve our bags, then pass through customs. And of course I couldn't get a signal on my cell phone so I couldn't book a car yet.

"We need to change Leo's diaper," I said while we waited at the baggage carousel. "And I really need to pee." I was five months pregnant and was shocked I hadn't already peed my pants. I could normally only hold it about thirty minutes.

"OK, I'll stay here and wait for the bags," Mika offered.

I hustled Leo to the bathroom where the world's longest line greeted me. Crap. We needed to snag a rental car before the rest of the airport had the same idea. I couldn't afford to wait an hour.

"Back so soon?" Mika asked, still no luggage.

"The line reached all the way to hell. I'll just hold it and I guess Leo's fine for now."

The bags trundled out an hour later. If I'd have known it would take that long, I would have waited for the bathroom!

We breezed through customs and were greeted by an airline representative.

"How can I help you?" he asked.

"Hi, sir. We are rebooked on a flight for Wednesday but we live close enough to drive. If we skip this leg of our trip is the rest of our ticket still valid?"

I wanted to verify this before we blew $2,000 worth of international travel, especially since I'd heard airlines invalidate the rest of your flight if you miss a leg. Apparently it's to deter people from booking a cheaper round-trip flight when they're only planning to use one portion.

"You'll have to ask an agent in Terminal 3."

"Which terminal are we in?"

"Five. You have to take the tram to Terminal 3. Except the tram isn't working because of the cold. But there should be a bus running. Head out these double doors here, then follow the crowd."

Mika took the luggage while I handled the stroller and our carry-ons. We waited patiently by the exit, freezing our noses off every time the automatic doors opened. Minus 11 degrees was bad enough, but the arctic wind chill dropped it to 25 below zero. Leo started to cry, probably from a combination of stress, hunger, and the cold. Great.

A bus with a sign taped to the side, on which was scrawled Terminal 3, pulled up across the street. A horde of people scrambled out of the building, climbing over each other to board. The bus drove away with doors open and people hanging off the back, leaving a crowd on the curb that looked just as large as the initial crowd.

Were these people going to wait outside for the next bus? My asthmatic son surely wouldn't be able to last more than a minute, and honestly, neither could I. My contacts would freeze to my eyeballs. How would I ever get on the bus? There would always be a group of people more desperate than us who'd endure the cold to ensure they got on the next bus.

We weren't making it to Terminal 3.

I whipped out my phone and searched for a signal while Mika tended to a crying Leo.

"Mom? It's me. Not much time to talk. We're stuck

in Chicago until Wednesday unless I can get a car out of here. Could you—"

"Wednesday! But I want to see my grandbaby!"

"Mom, no time. And don't you want to see us, too? Never mind, no time. Can you please call the airline and check to see if we void our tickets by driving this leg instead of flying? I'm going to try to rent a car. I'll call you back in five."

I hung up before she could ask how Leo was doing. We had to hurry, even if it meant being rude to my mom for a few minutes. She would understand.

I spotted a bank of ancient telephones with signs overhead advertising hotels and car rental agencies. Bingo.

"Mika, I'm going over there to call the car rental place. You got Leo?"

"Yep!" Leo had settled down but was still clearly out of his element. The airport was frigid, the bottle Mika had tried to give him was cold, and I'm sure his diaper was nice and warm. But what could we do? The entire airport was crowded, making it impossible to go to the bathroom or heat a baby bottle in under an hour, and we needed to be ready to dash off at a moment's notice.

The phone area was utter chaos. One phone was broken and the others were occupied. Two groups were ahead of me—a pair of college-aged girls and a family of four—but the rest were a scattered mess of idiots. Some were checking the arrivals screen above the hotel ads, others were drifting aimlessly. All of them stood between me and my escape route—the phones—and so they all posed a threat.

I tried to keep cool but some moron butted in front of me. It was bad enough I had to wait while cars were being snatched from beneath my nose, but I sure as heck wasn't going to let somebody cut in line.

In France, where situations like this happen on a daily

basis, I control my rage because it's not my country and not my language. I don't want to be the crazy foreigner shouting in broken French at a bunch of strangers.

But we were in my country now and my compatriots were acting like a bunch of fools. I couldn't take it anymore.

"People, people!" I shouted. "This madness has to stop. Who's in line? Raise your hand."

The crowd turned to look at the shouting crazy lady but no one raised their hand.

"I mean business, folks. I need to get my family out of this hellhole and this pathetic excuse for a line isn't helping. Raise your hand if you're in line or else you just lost your place."

Blank stares.

"Alright, I'll do it for you. You two," I said, pointing at the college girls. "You're next. After you is this family. Then it's me. If anyone else even tries to butt in front of me, I will murder you."

A petite redhead meekly held up her hand. "Um, I was in line too."

"OK, then step right up. Though you might want to reconsider your definition of a line." I looked around for any other issues. "You, sir. Are you waiting for the phones?"

A clueless Asian guy turned around. "Um, I watch screen."

"Excellent. Step to the left and you can look as long as you like. Anyone else checking the monitors? Step to the left! I want one straight line for the phones. Got it?"

People queued up behind me while the stragglers pulled over to the side to check the arrivals screen. Was that so hard?

As I waited in my military-precision line, I remembered I needed to call Mom back.

"Hi honey, how's it going?"

"I yelled at half the airport, I have to pee, and Leo is on the verge of a breakdown. But Mika is holding it together. One out of three ain't bad." I waved over at my husband and son. "How about you? Did you get a hold of the airline?"

"Yep, and I did you one better. First, the airline said it's no problem for you to drive. You just have to call them later to reconfirm your tickets."

No problem, we could do that once we were safe and sound in St. Louis. "Thanks. And what's the other thing?"

"Doug booked you a car with Hertz. You just have to find a bus to take you to their lot and give them this confirmation number. You have a pen?"

With my phone (and patience) cutting in and out, it took a few tries to note the impossibly long confirmation number, but I got it. "Thank you both so much. Oh shoot, I see a Hertz bus pulling up. Gotta go!"

I ran over to Mika, leaving my perfectly formed line of people wondering why I'd made such a fuss only to leave two seconds later. Screw 'em.

"Mika, we gotta catch that bus. Go, go!"

He'd been holding Leo to keep him calm and I knew we wouldn't have time to buckle him back in and still make the bus. If Leo doesn't want to be in the stroller, he does The Plank and remains stick-straight so that there's no way to wedge him in without breaking his legs.

Mika ran with Leo in one arm, dragging a suitcase with the other. I tossed the carry-ons into the stroller, pushing it with one hand (which caused it to veer wildly out of control), while dragging the other suitcase behind me.

The sidewalk and road were icy and the bitter cold air froze me to the bone the second I stepped outside. Mika made it on the bus, which was on the other side of the road, but I still had about 50 feet to cover. It's hard for a five-months-pregnant lady to run very fast on ice, particularly when weighed down by bags.

"Wait! Wait!" I shouted. The bus started to drive away with my husband and son on it, but the doors were still open. "Wait you *bleep-er bleepin'* bus! I'm five *bleeping* months pregnant and my *bleeping* family is on that *bleeping* bus!"

After my eloquent speech, the bus driver stopped. I tossed the luggage and stroller on and flew up the stairs.

"Good evening, everyone," I said with a smile, smoothing my hair. "Thank you for waiting," I said to the bus driver.

"Nice move, Mama," Mika said. "I was afraid he was going to leave without you! I tried to get him to stop but I guess he didn't hear me."

Well, he—and the entire airport—certainly heard *me*!

৽৵

The bus arrived at the car rental lot. We were almost on our way.

Due to the severe cold, all the cars in the lot were already turned on. So wasteful, so American, so helpful. Because otherwise the doors would freeze shut and render the cars unusable.

A few papers to sign and we'd be *en route*. I chitchatted with the guy at the desk while Mika installed the car seat. I commended the Hertz employee for braving the cold and working in such crappy weather. Their outpost was heated with only one dinky space heater and they didn't even have a bathroom. Which sucked for me and my full bladder but must have really sucked for them.

"So where do you guys go to the bathroom?"

"We have to walk across the lot to the main office."

"In this cold?"

Right then Mika burst through the door. "I'm sorry but I can't figure out the car seat. And my feet are frozen." His thin Converse shoes didn't stand up against the snow and freezing temperatures.

"I'll help you sir," the desk agent volunteered. In France they would have said "That's not our job," and sat behind the desk drinking coffee while you slowly lost one limb after another to frostbite.

Soon enough, we were on our way. Leo, his diaper weighing more than him now, passed out immediately in the back seat.

"Here we go!" I cheered, pulling out of the lot. "It's normally about five hours to St. Louis, but since we're already outside the city, it might even be faster!"

It wasn't.

The roads were paved in slick ice, and roadside notification boards urged travelers to "Only travel if necessary. Roads in dangerous condition."

I averaged about 40 miles per hour, taking cues from the truckers on the road. If I saw their brakes light up in the distance ahead, I had ample time to slow down before hitting the rough patch. If they were sailing smoothly, I allowed myself to accelerate to the luxurious speed of 60 miles per hour. At this rate, the journey would take seven hours. Add in the time difference with Paris and it would feel like driving until 9:00 am.

"We should stop for coffee," I suggested. "Plus Mama needs to pee."

"You don't have to tell me twice!" Mika said.

Here's the thing I love about America (apart from my Hertz Hero): We were in the middle of a snowstorm and the lowest temperatures the Chicago area had seen in 30 years, yet the gas stations were open with freshly brewed coffee and fresh-enough donuts. The bathrooms were decently clean and didn't cost a dime.

We took turns running into the shop, not wanting to

wake Leo up or remove him from the warmth of the car. That also meant we missed another opportunity for a diaper change. If I wasn't careful, I'd get pulled over for being the world's worst parent.

ꕔ

"Isn't that the saddest story you've ever heard?" I said, wiping the tears from my eyes.

Two coffee breaks later, we were about 30 minutes away from my mom's house. We'd passed the long hours by telling embarrassing stories from our younger days, and then somehow I got on the subject of how *The Time Traveler's Wife* was the best yet saddest book I'd ever read. So sad that I brought myself to tears just talking about it.

I really needed to sleep.

Right about then, my precious angel in the back seat woke up. I couldn't believe he'd made it that long. Poor guy had had a rough 24 hours. And now he was pissed off.

"What should we do, Mika? We have to keep him in his car seat. You want to try feeding him?"

"From the front?"

"Can you hop in the back?"

"While we're driving?"

"I really don't want to stop if we don't have to. It's already 1:30 in the morning. I just want to get home. We're almost there."

My 6'4" husband squeezed between the seats and landed on the back seat as gracefully as a drunk on a banana peel. He tried to give Leo a cold bottle. No dice. Seconds later, cookies flew past me and landed on the dashboard. I guess he didn't want those either.

"The wheels on the bus go round and round, round and round," I started. Leo instantly calmed. Great! I could do this the rest of the ride if I had to!

I had to.

Thirty minutes later we pulled into my parents' driveway as I sung the last made-up chorus of the song I now hated. "The mommy in the car is going crazy, going crazy, going crazy!"

Mom rushed out in her pajamas to greet us while Doug unloaded our luggage.

"You made it!" she said, giving us hugs and kisses. "Now let me see my sweet grandson."

"No problem. First order of business—you can change his diaper."

Apple Crumble

There's something about air travel that makes people order ginger ale. Have you noticed that? You never hear people talk much about ginger ale, until Seat 4C requests it and creates a ripple effect throughout the whole plane. Maybe there's something soothing and stomach-settling about it, which is why it makes the perfect ingredient for this travel-disaster-inspired cocktail.

1 oz. dark rum
3 oz. apple juice
1 oz. ginger ale

1. Fill a highball glass halfway with ice.
2. Add rum, apple juice, and ginger ale.
3. Stir slowly and then drink even more slowly. We don't want any upset tummies around here.

Makes 1 serving

A Season of Love

Dating and engagement and marriage, oh my!

17

Something to Prove

Strolling the streets of the City of Light, it was apparent the holiday season was upon us. The French don't shy away from Christmas decorations the way many overly politically correct American establishments do. The town is covered in light displays and greenery and nativity scenes, all with a certain Parisian chic to them.

As charming as it was, I bid *adieu* for a few weeks to visit both sets of parents in the U.S.

"I'm looking forward to heading home for the holidays," I said to my friend Anne Marie over a pint of cider at the bar she worked at. "But I can't imagine being away from Mika for two whole weeks."

"What, are you two's joined at the hip, you are?" she teased in her Irish accent. "It'll do you good to get away from each other for a while before you turn into a couple of old married farts."

I gulped down my drink, afraid she might be right. Would I become lame now that I had a serious boyfriend? Or would I keep my Party Girl identity, the one who danced on tabletops and passed out on bathroom floors? Or would this be the perfect chance to find some balance in my life, perhaps keeping the tabletop-dancing but nixing the bathroom-floor-sleeping?

The night before my trip, we all went out partying. It started out innocently enough, but the events that followed changed my partying policy forever—I no longer allow myself to drink the night before an international flight.

I simply can't be trusted.

But that night I didn't know or didn't care. I wanted to prove that, yeah, OK, maybe I was spending a lot of time with my new beau but I could still party with the best of them. I was young and cool, not old and married.

I went a tad overboard with my point-proving. If by "tad" I mean "so far overboard even a lifeboat couldn't save me."

Let's not share exactly how much I drank or else my mom might check me into rehab, but let's just say it rhymes with Schmoo Bottles of Schmampagne and Schmour Shots.

"Hey babe, I don't mean to be a drag, but shouldn't we be getting home?" Mika dared to ask. "It's nearly 4:00 and you have to be up in a few hours."

I shot him a look that could kill. "What? Who cares! Let's live for tonight and worry about tomorrow tomorrow. Now where are those shots?"

Make that Schmoo Bottles of Schmampagne and Schmive Shots.

∿∿

The next morning (or three hours later, take your

pick), I heard a knock on my door. *Go away, I don't want any.*

More persistent knocking. "What?" I wondered aloud, lugging myself out of bed. "Ohhhhhhhh, fudge. That must be Mika."

I answered the door to my boyfriend's shocked expression. "Um, we need to go but do you maybe want to take a shower first?"

Glancing in the mirror, I saw what he meant. I looked as bad as I felt, which was horrible. "Yeah, I'll just be a minute."

Fifteen minutes later, I was somehow showered and dressed, though I'm sure I missed a few spots. It's hard to reach everywhere when you're leaning against the shower wall.

Faking like I felt better than I did, so as not to let him know he had been right the night before, I grabbed my purse. "OK, I'm ready to go. Do you want me to drive?"

He had borrowed his parents' car to take me to the airport and I thought that by driving I might feel less queasy.

"Um...." he stalled.

"What?" I asked, flinging my arm out to make a point. However, in doing so my purse knocked over a chair, landing on the floor in a loud thud. Whoops. Maybe the alcohol hadn't completely worn off yet.

"No offense, but maybe you're not totally sober? I don't mind driving."

Man, this guy was good. How had he not said "I told you so" yet? I would have been rubbing that in his face if the roles were reversed. Though they never would be— he would never be so irresponsible.

"Good idea. You drive. Let's go then?"

"After you," he said, picking up my suitcase.

It took me forever to walk down the five awful flights of stairs in my apartment building. This was going to be a long ride. I had to say it. "You were right, you know. We should have gone home when you said so. Probably even sooner."

He let out a smile before quickly covering it up. "Well, we all have our nights like that."

He never had nights like that but I didn't want to make myself look any worse. He had let me off the hook without rubbing it in, which was way more than I deserved.

༽ঙ্গ

As bad as I felt, it paled in comparison to what happened once I boarded the plane. Warning: graphic vomit scenes up ahead. If you can't handle it, I suggest you skip a few pages or visualize puppies running through a field.

Before passing security, I bought a sandwich (salami and pickle, which I would regret in the very near future) and we sat on the floor while I tried to eat it. The airport was spinning. How would I endure a 10-hour flight? Thinking about it made my stomach turn.

"Sorry I'm so hungover," I said to Mika. "But now we don't have to worry about a drawn-out tearful goodbye. I can't even hold my head up for longer than two seconds."

"Are you going to be OK?" he asked, his concern showing clearly on his face.

"Do I have a choice?"

"Good point. Well, try not to think about it," he said, rubbing my back. "I'm going to miss you while you're gone, but at least I'll finally get to bed at a reasonable hour." He looked at me with an amused smile, one I was growing quite accustomed to by now.

"Ha, ha. You'll miss me more than you can imagine, Lesage, just wait and see."

༄༅

After finishing the last bite of my poor choice of a sandwich, I headed to security. Mika and I said a final goodbye, then continued to wave to each other the entire time I waited in line. Sweet, but it was making me dizzy.

A too-short-while later, I was buckled in my seat and not feeling any better. Ready for the longest, most painful flight of my life. Knowing the hangover was all my fault didn't help.

"You will find your flight information card in the seat back pocket in front of you," the flight attendant announced, rattling off a slew of other safety instructions.

Speaking of the seat back pocket in front of me, I should look for a barf bag. The salami and pickle sandwich (Seriously? What had I been thinking?) threatened to make an appearance and I needed to be prepared.

I rummaged through the pocket, finding the in-flight magazine, SkyMall, and the safety card, but no barf bag. A victim of airline cutbacks. Well, maybe I wouldn't need it.

My stomach churned as we taxied for what seemed like hours. *Are we driving there or flying? Get a move on!* I tried not to think about how sick I felt, but it was pretty much the only thing on my mind. Puppies running in fields transformed into puking puppies running in fields. Ice cream sundaes turned into puke-cream sundaes.

OK, let's think. We could only taxi for so long before the beast eventually had to take flight. From that point I only had to wait until the fasten seat belt sign was turned off and then I could rush to the toilet. Ew. Throwing up in an airplane restroom? What a terrifying thought.

If I only knew how the day would end, I would have

been begging for the chance to throw up in an airplane restroom.

I counted the rows to the lavatory. Eight. Could have been better but could have been worse. *I just have to make it ten more minutes, then run five seconds, and I'm safe. I can spend as much time as I need once I'm locked in the stall, I just need to make it there.*

The guy in the seat next to me darted surreptitious glances my way. I guess I did look suspicious, rifling through the seat back pocket and scoping out the plane. Did he think I had some sinister plan to take down the aircraft? Or could he simply tell from the green hue of my skin that something horrific was brewing?

I smiled weakly and tried to keep the vomit at bay. *2, 3, 5, 7, 11... uh oh.* My nifty trick to count prime numbers (I told you I was a math nerd) couldn't stop the inevitable. The vomit was making its way up and there was no stopping it.

To this day, I wonder why I didn't get up and run to the restroom. True, it's a violation of airplane security but surely that would have been better than what happened next.

By now you're thinking, "So what? She pukes on a plane. I saw this coming a mile away." Did you, Smarty Pants? Well, let's just say the first draft of this story was way more gruesome. But due to some loving editors who care about your sensibilities, we've decided to end the story here. If you want details, imagine the worst scenario possible and multiply it by 10, and then you'll get what I *wish* happened. Multiply it by 10 more and you'll be close to what did happen.

Let's fast forward, shall we?

∽∾

The rest of the flight passed slowly, giving me plenty

of time to regret my decisions from the night before. What had I been trying to prove? That I could party like I used to? I never used to do *this*. This was way over the top. Sure, it had been fun in the moment, but was definitely not worth the resulting pukefest-slash-hangover.

And I hadn't even gotten to say a proper goodbye to Mika! Half-heartedly waving while trying not to throw up was not the romantic way I'd hoped to part before the holidays.

That's it, I decided. *Just because I have a boyfriend doesn't mean I'm lame. Why had I thought it would?* I could still party, but I didn't have to party "like the good ol' days." Mika and I could go out sometimes, stay home sometimes. What mattered was that we were happy together. And we were. I had nothing to prove.

"Here you go, honey," the flight attendant said as she handed me a packet of pretzels and ginger ale. Accepting them gratefully, I realized all I had to prove was that I could make it the rest of the flight without vomiting on anyone. After that, it might be time to settle down a bit.

Or at least drink fewer than two bottles of champagne and five shots in one night.

Champagne Cocktail Classique

For me, there's no such thing as too much champagne. While other people count their consumption by the glass, I often count mine by the bottle. But sometimes (my mom would say *all the time*), it's better to slow down and enjoy your drinks. It'll make tomorrow's 10-hour flight that much easier.

sugar cube
dash of Angostura bitters
champagne
maraschino cherry

1.   Drop the sugar cube into a champagne flute.
2.   Add a dash of Angostura bitters and swirl.
3.   Pour champagne almost to the top.
4.   Garnish with a festive maraschino cherry, and savor the cocktail, knowing you have nothing to prove.

Makes 1 serving

18

Goodbye, Twenties

Before I knew it, my 30th birthday crept around the corner. Yikes. Thirty?

I was in a pretty good place—awesome relationship, decent apartment, pretty cool work-at-home gig. But I couldn't help comparing myself to my friends back home. Many of them were married, owned houses, and had bigshot jobs. Not that it was a competition, and clearly taking a few years out to live in Paris had affected my timeline, but I wondered if I was moving too slowly.

"So what do you want for your birthday?" Mika asked.

"Nothing, really. After last year's trip to Iceland, I'm set for life!" Though I could think of one thing I wanted. "But, um, like, maybe not for my birthday but maybe sometime kind of soon I would want, um, a ring?"

"A ring? What kind of ring?"

"You know, a *ring*," I said, looking into his eyes.

"Ah, I see. A *ring*. Well, your birthday is a bit soon, but what about Christmas? Or New Year's?"

Wow. Was this really happening? Talking about marriage? You mean I could actually broach the subject with my boyfriend, as opposed to waiting three years and then ransacking a suitcase behind his back (which I might or might not have done with Pierre)? Mika's willingness to discuss it was refreshing.

"Surprise me," I said. "I don't want to rob a Frenchman of his chance to be romantic. But I'm happy we're on the same page."

ড়়ঌ

Headed home for the holidays, this year I was sober as could be. Lesson officially learned. No more throwing up on planes. And now I was able to say a sufficiently sappy goodbye to my future fiancé before dying a slow death in the endless security line.

"I'm going to miss you," I said, hugging him around the waist.

"It's only for a week. Then I'll be there, too," Mika replied, kissing the top of my head. "Time will fly, don't worry. And as soon as you get to Taco Bell, you'll forget all about me."

He had a point. I could almost taste the Double Decker Taco Supreme as he spoke. "I'll call you when I land," I said, giving him a kiss.

"You better," he said with a smile, as we finally broke away from each other.

We could be stars in the world's cheesiest chick flick if we went on any longer.

ড়়ঌ

A week later, my stomach was in a flurry. Mom and I

had baked a ton of Christmas cookies that morning and I'd eaten way more raw dough than I should have.

"It's all the sugar," I said to her.

"Are you sure it's not because a certain someone is arriving today?" she asked. It was December 26th, so if Mika stuck to his word (and I had every reason to believe he would), I would be engaged within the next five days. No wonder I was hyped up.

"How am I going to make it until 5:00? That's ages from now!" I whined. I may have been thirty years old but that didn't stop me from acting like a kid around my mom.

"Well, definitely don't eat any more cookies or you'll be even more wound up," she said.

❦

At last 5:00 arrived and I borrowed Mom's car to pick up my beau at the airport. The 20-minute drive felt like an eternity. The overhead monitors said he'd arrive in the C concourse, so I waited outside the security exit by the C gates. The next 30 minutes were agony.

I paced back and forth.

I hopped from foot to foot.

I counted floor tiles. I counted ceiling tiles.

I had just started reciting prime numbers when I saw a tall head bobbing out of the corner of my eye.

He was here!

We stared at each other, goofy smiles on our faces as he closed the distance. Once he was out of the concourse, he scooped me up in a bear hug.

"That was the longest week of my life!" I said.

"I know! I missed you too. But I'm here now," he said, giving me a smoochy kiss.

Noticing some prudish onlookers, I cut the smooch-fest short. "Enough mushy stuff. Let's get your bags."

We walked hand-in-hand to baggage claim.

I was super excited to see Mika but an itty bitty part of me was let down that he hadn't proposed to me yet. *Chill, woman*, I thought. *Let the man breathe the St. Louis air before you jump on his case!* I'd assumed the ring would be burning a hole in his pocket during the flight and that he'd want to unload it as soon as possible. And since we'd be surrounded by family the rest of the trip, I'd thought he'd want to get it over with at the airport. That's not very romantic, though. *Again, woman, chill. He'll do it when he's ready.*

"Luggage from Flight 2314 will be arriving on Carousel 4," an announcement blared.

"That's my flight," Mika said, as he steered me to a sign with a large number four on it. He scanned the room in every direction. I glanced around to see what he was looking at. Why was he being so weird? When I turned back to him, he was holding a ring.

Ohmygod. It's happening!

"It may not be romantic, but my hands are sweaty from gripping this thing so tightly ever since I left Paris. I'm afraid it's going to fly out of my hands if I wait any longer. And anyway, since our first date, we've always talked about travel and then we actually went on all the trips we said we would. So airports are kind of our thing. And it shows that when we say we'll do something, we do it. I'd love to travel with you the rest of my life. I'm rambling. I'm kind of nervous. Anyway, will you marry me?"

Could he be any more adorable? "Yes!" I shouted. "Of course I will! Now let me help you out by taking that ring off your hands."

He handed over the entire ring box, hands shaking. I wanted to slip on the ring but first I gave him a huge hug, and then a not-so-short kiss. Puritan bystanders be damned, I just got engaged! I'm entitled to a public display of affection.

I felt him calm down in my arms. "Don't worry, now it's my ring to lose. You can relax," I said with a smile, sliding the ring on my finger.

"Do you like it? I picked it out by myself. I wasn't sure if it was your style."

"It's perfect," I assured him. Though I was so in love I would have found beauty in a Fruit Loop. "I hope your bags come out soon. I can't wait to tell everyone the news!"

ॐॐ

I tried not to stare at my brand-new ring as I drove us to the Christmas party for Doug's side of the family.

"I'm gonna give my dad a quick call," I said to Mika. Because talking on the phone while driving is way safer than admiring a ring.

"Cool, I'll call my parents at the same time."

It was the middle of the night when Catherine and Gilbert picked up the phone, but they were thrilled with the news. "*Félicitations!*" they called down the line.

At the same time, my dad offered his congratulations. "And good luck to Mika, he's really in for it." Hey! What's that supposed to mean?

The party was more of the same. "Congratulations, but watch out, she's a live one!"

OK, I know I can be feisty and Mika is famously calm, but he knows what he's getting into. And if he doesn't, then shhhh, don't tell him!

Chambord Vodka Lemonade

My engagement to Mika marked the merging of two cultures, French and American. This recipe blends the classy French side (Chambord) with a classic American beverage (lemonade), and throws in a little vodka for good measure.

1 oz. Chambord
1 oz. vodka
3 oz. lemonade
lime wedge

1. Pour Chambord, vodka, and lemonade in a tall glass with ice.
2. Garnish with a lime wedge and wait to see which holiday surprises come your way.

Makes 1 serving

19

Eau de Cologne

OK, so you know Mika ends up proposing to me. But you knew that before you even started reading this book because my last name is *très* French. Spoiler alert: We get married and have two kids. Or at least we had two kids at the time of writing this. Oh dear God I hope we don't have any more because I'm already enough of a walking zombie as it is. Although if we do have more kids, and one of those kids is reading this years in the future, I want you to know how very much I love you and how I always wanted you and you were not an accident at all, despite what you thought you overheard Mommy saying to Daddy the other day.

Right. So after my little 30th birthday freak-out, Mika promised we would get engaged before the end of the year. And because I overanalyze everything and because I don't like surprises and because I'm the opposite of romantic, I spent nearly every day before December 31st looking for clues to see if that day would be the day he'd propose.

"Hi honey, I'm on my way home," Mika said on one of our nightly post-work phone calls.

"Cool! Can't wait to see you. Do you mind picking up a baguette?"

He opened the front door, one hand behind his back, and said, "Hi sweetie. I have a surprise for you."

Oh my freaking God, it's happening. Right now. I was cooking spaghetti and red sauce was splattered all over my face and he was going to propose RIGHT NOW. Ahhhhhhhhhhhhhhh!

He pulled his arm from behind his back and offered me a *tarte au chocolat.* "For dessert. I picked it up while I was getting the baguette."

I couldn't be angry. The guy had brought me baked goods. It doesn't get much better than that. And I wasn't even disappointed that he hadn't proposed. Did I really expect him to propose on a cold and rainy weeknight? Well, Parisian winters were always cold and rainy so I guess I'd have to expect he would do it on a cold and rainy day, but maybe not amidst the after-work rush.

I really needed to chill out and just forget about it. He promised he would do it before the end of the year. I had to trust him. I had to not ruin every moment with the anticipation of a proposal. And I had to stop splattering spaghetti sauce everywhere.

"What do you think about going to Cologne this year?"

We'd started a tradition (well, we'd done it once so far, but you have to start somewhere) of going to Germany during the holiday season to visit the Christmas markets. Several plazas in the city center housed adorable temporary wooden shops that sold handmade Christmas gifts and decorations. I enjoyed browsing the stands, but couldn't buy anything—I had no room in my apartment for tchotchkes.

But I did have room in my belly for goodies from the food stands. Soft, warm pretzels. Glühwein, or mulled wine, to take the chill off the crisp air. Hamburgers and bratwursts. More soft pretzels. More Glühwein.

"Count me in!"

"Great. I'll check train fares and see what sort of discount I can get at work."

Mika worked at a four-star hotel chain and could usually score amazing discounts when we traveled. If we were willing to stay at a lower-end hotel, we could pay next to nothing. If we wanted a swanky, high-end hotel, we could get a rate that put it in our price range. Either way, we would have plenty of money left over for copious amounts of Glühwein.

A few days later, everything was booked. We were staying at a swanky hotel.

Could this be when he was going to pop the question?

ﯤﯤ

"What do you want to do today?" Mika asked over the bountiful hotel brunch buffet.

"I dunno. Maybe walk around a bit, then eat some pretzels and drink some Glühwein."

He didn't even bat an eyelash. Many people would balk at the thought of talking about your next meal while you were still working on your first. Not us. Our vacations were all about eating, walking, eating, walking, then eating and walking some more. I could save myself a lot of time and trouble and just order delivery to my treadmill, but I guess that's not very "international" or "glamorous" or "actually even a vacation."

"I noticed one of the Christmas markets has an ice skating rink. Do you want to go skating?"

What a lovely idea! Ever since the first time I watched the Olympics on TV as a little girl, I've loved figure skating. How could you not? Sparkly outfits and leaping through the air? Yes, please!

Of course, that wasn't what happened when *I* skated. Bundled in about 50 layers of clothing (both to combat the cold and to pad against the inevitable falls), you could barely see my figure. Which was just as well considering the number of pretzels I'd consumed.

We strolled through the quaint streets of Cologne, enjoying the sights and smells. Mmm, the smells.

Since it was still relatively early in the day, the line for the skating rink wasn't too long. We approached the ticket seller. "*Swie*, uh, tickets, *bitte*," Mika said.

"Two tickets? Yes, here you go," the ticket seller replied. Mika and I liked to try out our horrible German, but since most Germans speak English, they prefer to get straight to the point and use the most efficient language. *Nein* problem.

"Oh, and can I get a locker, too?" Mika asked.

A locker? The other skaters had piled their shoes next to the benches that lined the rink, figuring no one would steal a stranger's stinky old shoes.

"Why do you want a locker?" I asked Mika.

"I don't want to skate with my bag."

I hadn't noticed he'd brought his satchel with him until now. Don't worry, it wasn't a purse or a European man bag. It was a manly messenger bag covered in Beatles patches. Not that there's anything wrong with man bags (besides everything).

He often brought the bag with him on vacation so he could stash water bottles and guide books, but we hadn't brought water bottles and guide books. So why did he have his bag with him? Was, maybe, my ring in there? And why was I being so nosy?

We changed into our skates. "Here, hand me your

shoes," Mika said. "I'm going to the lockers. Why don't you go on ahead to the rink? I'll meet you there."

Yes! This was totally it! I walked awkwardly, as you do when you're crossing wooden planks while wearing ice skates, over to the rink. I glanced back and saw Mika fumbling with something in his satchel. I looked away. Maybe I should give him some privacy and leave a little room for surprise.

But man oh man was this going to be good! Being proposed to while ice skating in Cologne!

As if on cue, a few snowflakes drifted down from the sky. *You've got to be kidding me. This is perfect!*

I started a lap while Mika finished whatever it was he was doing. I whizzed around like Kristi Yamaguchi, if Kristi Yamaguchi had banana peels glued to her skates. But I didn't care. I was marrying the world's most perfect man, and he was going to propose to me any second now!

I finished my lap just as Mika entered the rink.

"Hi there, stranger," I said, in what I meant to be a sultry voice but came out all squealy and high-pitched because I was so excited.

"Hi! Shall we?" He took my hand in his and started skating, clearly with as many banana peels under his skates as me.

During the long, clumsy lap he kept looking in my eyes and smiling, but didn't say anything. Maybe he was nervous. That made sense. Perhaps I should help him out. Yeah, actually, that's totally what I should do. Think about it. His tall frame was already quite wobbly on skates. He wasn't going to propose *while* skating. What had I been thinking? He would need to pull off to the side, distract me for a second, and *then* get the ring out. And clearly he was having trouble figuring out a good time and place to stop. He probably thought I was enjoying skating instead of analyzing his every move. I had to jump in and save him from himself! Knowing him, he would break out in cold sweats soon due to nerves. I couldn't do that to the man I loved. The man I was going to marry!

"Hey, you want to pull over and take a break?" I asked casually.

"Already?" he asked, but he was visibly relieved. I *knew* it.

"Yeah, maybe let's just stop over there in the corner. Take a breath, enjoy the view."

We skated over and came to a stop. I played it cool by looking around at the market, giving him time to pull the ring out of his pocket. Then I turned back, eyes sparkling with anticipation. I mean, I couldn't see the sparkle in my own eyes but I felt it. I was READY.

And then... nothing. He gave me a goofy grin, then grabbed my hand. "OK, ready to go? I could use some Glühwein. My hands are freezing."

What the...? I was so sure I'd been right! All the signs were there. How come he hadn't proposed?

I skated along like I wasn't bothered. Because I wasn't. No, not at all. He still had a month to propose and I was on vacation in a delightful city. I didn't have to get engaged. I didn't have to scrutinize every little movement. I could just relax and enjoy my weekend.

I couldn't just relax. "So, uh, hey, honey? How come you got a locker? Are you sure there wasn't anything in your bag?" Great, now I'd turned into my dad, firing off three questions in a row.

Mika looked understandably perplexed, trying to decide which question to answer. He settled on a clever, "Huh?"

"Well, ha ha, actually, this is so silly, but I kind of thought you were going to propose." His eyes widened. I should have stopped talking but I couldn't. "I saw you fumbling with your bag and I thought you were hiding the ring and I thought maybe you would propose while we were skating even though that's crazy but it's romantic so maybe it's just crazy romantic but... Oh my God, maybe you're going to do it now? Maybe I'm ruining it? Or maybe you were going to do it later and I'm still ruining it? Or maybe I should just shut u—"

"Shh," he said gently, wrapping his arms around me. "You haven't ruined anything. If you must know, I ordered the ring but it won't arrive for a few more weeks. So I won't be proposing this weekend. If you let me," he gave me a knowing look here, and not for the first time in our relationship, "I'll try to surprise you at some point. Try, being the operative word here, Sherlock."

I should have felt sheepish but I didn't. I was just happy to be having such an open, honest conversation with the man I loved. "Yes, that sounds great. I'll stop being so nosy."

"Good."

"So why were you fumbling in your bag?"

"I thought you were going to stop being nosy? That didn't last long."

"Oh please. You know me."

"And you know me. I fumble. I'm clumsy. But you still love me." He smiled.

"It's what I love most about you. That, and everything else."

"Perfect. Glühwein?"

"Perfect."

Glühwein

If you can't make it to Germany (or Austria) for their famous winter markets, you can still enjoy this warm-you-to-the-core beverage in the comfort of your cozy home.

2 bottles red wine
2 cups water
6 cloves
2 cinnamon sticks
2 oranges, cut into chunks

1. Combine all ingredients in a pot and bring almost to a boil. Let simmer.
2. Serve with a slotted spoon to avoid clove and cinnamon sticks getting into the glasses (but keep them in the pot for flavor).
3. Best served in slightly warmed mugs to keep the chill of winter far away.

Makes 8-10 servings

The Holiday Blues

Maybe they should change the name to Sickmas

20

All I Want For Christmas Is
My Two Front Teeth

I'm mildly obsessed with teeth. That's what happens when you have not one but two traumatic dental experiences.

When I was a kid, I fell off a row of bleachers and knocked out my two front teeth.

I totally deserved it.

My mom and I picked up Stephen from basketball practice and I tormented him as usual. I chased him up the bleachers, then shouted, "First one down wins! Last one's a loser!"

As it was the middle of winter, I was wearing my snazzy high-heeled snow boots. I was 11. I had no business wearing high-heeled snow boots. I also had no business running up and down bleachers in said snow boots.

Knowing I would never defeat my speedy brother by

running down the bleachers, I opted to jump off the side instead. One of my heels got caught on the edge and I face-planted on the basketball court. It hurt so bad it almost didn't hurt at all.

Blood splattered everywhere. Girls screamed and guys said stuff like "Dude, is that Steve's sister?" and "Some girl broke her face."

Hey, that's MY face you're talking about!

My mom rushed over, helped me up, and escorted me to the bathroom.

The moment of truth: looking in the mirror. I thought maybe I'd broken my nose or busted my lip. But no, one of my front teeth was loose and a huge piece of the other one had chipped off.

An image came to my head, of future me in a wood-paneled boardroom trying to convince a CEO to agree to my marketing plan. My papers were prepared and I was dressed in a sharp suit. But the CEO just kept staring at my chipped tooth and wouldn't take me seriously[3].

That was it. My life was over. My career had ended before I'd even made it out of childhood.

Our family dentist, Dr. Sheinbein, fixed my smile a few days later. He did a decent job and his repairs lasted for years, even though upon close inspection (which I did way more than necessary) you could see my teeth weren't perfect.

In my late twenties, I decided to have them redone. X-rays showed that each tooth needed a root canal, and I could get pearly white crowns at the same time. And why

---

[3] I used this boardroom anecdote on my application for the second season of "The Apprentice," and made the cut of 50 interviewees selected out of 16,000 applicants in the Midwest. I didn't make it past the first round, but it was an amazing experience. So the whole losing-my-teeth episode wasn't all for nothing!

not throw in a little professional teeth whitening?

I'd booked an appointment with the cosmetic dentist Dr. Sheinbein had recommended and would be seeing him on my upcoming trip to the U.S. Much as I enjoyed Paris, I was looking forward to going home for the holidays, not just to fix my teeth and to see my family, but for a change of scenery since I'd recently broken up with my long-time French-Brazilian boyfriend, Pierre. While the break-up hadn't been traumatic, it still represented a big change in my life.

"Hello, Vicki! Come right this way and we'll get started." The dentist I'd be spending the next five hours with was friendly and welcoming. He whitened and molded and photographed. Then we were ready for the masterpiece to begin.

"Here's an iPod to help pass the time," his equally friendly assistant said.

I managed to kill half an hour just figuring out how the damn thing worked. I know how to program computers and I enjoy differential equations more than one should, but am clueless when it comes to these newfangled gadgets.

Once I finally got it to play, I tuned out as drills buzzed and whirred. I even fell asleep for a while.

When I woke up, I noticed the iPod had stopped. I'd been in the dentist's chair so long it had run out of batteries! Considering the cost of the dental work, I figured it was acceptable to ask for a recharge or another iPod. Who knew how much longer I'd be stuck there? Musical distraction was just what I needed.

"Ekthuse me, but thith ith out of batterieth," I spit out. Um, why did I sound like Daffy Duck? I don't know what I thought root canals and crowns were before I started the appointment, but feeling two metal spikes with my tongue, I suddenly realized I no longer had two front teeth. The teeth I'd known for more than two decades were gone, replaced by vampire fangs.

The dentist must have seen the expression of terror on my face, as he quickly reassured me, "Almost finished! All we have to do is slide the teeth on and you'll be on your way!"

So I guess they'd forgotten about the iPod. I had to endure the rest of the appointment acutely aware of the work being done in my mouth. I was fearful of the results.

"All done," he said, after what seemed like centuries, raising the chair to a seated position. "Let's have a look!"

He handed me a mirror, then stepped back, beaming with pride.

I hesitantly opened my mouth and smiled at my reflection.

Oh. My. God.

I'd thought nothing could be worse than my metal Dracula fangs but I'd been wrong. In their place were the fakest teeth I'd ever seen. First, they were slightly yellower than the rest of my teeth. Didn't we bleach my teeth for a reason? So that the crowns would be the same shade of sparkling white?

Second, they were gigantic. Way bigger than my old teeth. They practically needed their own zip code. I was one step away from Bugs Bunny.

But most importantly, my "teeth" were actually ONE BIG TOOTH WITH A LINE SCRATCHED DOWN THE MIDDLE to make it look like two teeth.

I'm not kidding.

I started to hyperventilate. I couldn't believe I'd been tortured for five hours to end up looking like a cartoon character.

"What do you think?" the dentist asked, oblivious to my concern. "They look great, huh?"

"Um, I have to go," I said, handing him the mirror, grabbing my purse and coat, and running the heck out of there.

I stopped by the front desk to pay, even though it seemed a crime to be charged for this.

"Hi honey," the smiling receptionist said. "Ooh, your teeth are beautiful! Your total is $4,567. Will you be paying by check or credit card?"

"Credit card," I squeaked. I was about to have a breakdown. Between the astronomical cost and the Bugs Bunny tooth (singular), I was on the verge of tears. Oh, please no, don't let me cry in the waiting room! But as soon as I thought about crying, the waterworks started up.

"Oh honey, what's the matter?" the receptionist asked, processing my credit card as slowly as humanly possible.

I had to get out of there. Why was this taking so long? And could I please stop crying?

In between sniffles I managed to reply. "I'm so upset with my tooth. It's ONE tooth and it's big and yellow and ugly. And expensive. And I wanted to look good now that I'm single because my boyfriend and I broke up!" I was wailing at that point.

Mercifully, she finished with my credit card and handed it back to me. "Well, if it makes you feel any better, my husband just died."

What? How would that make me feel better? Now instead of wallowing in misery over my first-world problem and expensive rabbit tooth, I had to come up with something sympathetic to say to this grieving widow.

"I'm really sorry to hear that. That must be tough," I mumbled. "I'm sorry, but I have to go." I grabbed my stuff and ran out the door, only then noticing the two other people in the waiting room. As if the ordeal hadn't been embarrassing enough, now there were witnesses!

In the end, it all worked out. What the dentist had

failed to tell me was that this tooth (I refuse to call it "teeth") was only temporary until my crowns came in. That's what all the molds and photos were about. I had to sport my Bugs Bunny tooth for the longest two weeks of my life, but eventually, I was the proud owner of two shiny, white, perfectly shaped teeth.

Just in time for Christmas.

Peppermintini

How do you tie together Christmas and teeth? Peppermint, of course. The Peppermintini will get you in the Christmas mood while reminding you of your last fluoride treatment at the dentist. Wait, maybe that's not such a good idea. Anyway, the drink is delicious.

3 oz. Irish cream liqueur
1/2 oz. vodka
1/2 oz. peppermint schnapps
1 oz. milk

1. Add ingredients to a martini shaker filled with ice. Shake.
2. Strain into a martini glass and enjoy as it whitens your teeth*.

Makes 1 serving

*Does not actually whiten your teeth, but after a few of these you won't notice the color of your teeth anyway.

21

Emotion Sickness

The best laid plans usually get thrown up on.

I should have known our trip to the U.S. would be a disaster. The fact that I'd had to beg my boss to let me go. The fact that we'd be traveling with a four-month-old. The fact that airline ticket prices were exorbitant. So much was against us.

"I know it's tough honey, but we're all looking forward to seeing you," my mom said on the phone the night before our 18-hour door-to-door trip. "I've got everything ready. You won't have to lift a finger once you're here. You just focus on getting here in one piece."

After hanging up, I checked my travel planning spreadsheet, color-coded for each person in the family. We were all set for the following day. We just needed to wake up, shower, and head out the door.

The three of us slept peacefully in our cozy little room until the alarm went off at 5:00 a.m. Leo usually served as our alarm clock, so I'd completely forgotten the sound of our real one. I woke with a startle— "Someone's breaking in and trying to steal our baby!"— but then two seconds later our automatic coffee machine began to whir. Oh right, it's just morning. The morning of our trip!

We got ready in record time, allowing us to relax over coffee. I checked the travel planning spreadsheet again. "OK, so we should leave in about five minutes if we want to catch the 7:15 Air France bus," I said.

The Air France bus is this brilliant service that takes you to the airport for a reasonable price, even if you're not flying Air France. Seats are limited and only two buses run per hour, but it's a great deal if you get there on time. And while the bus only stops at three stations in all of Paris, one of those stops was a four-minute walk down our street. It really couldn't be easier.

Mika rounded up all our stuff and I carried Leo, about to follow Mika out the door. *We must be forgetting something. This is too easy. Passports, luggage, baby—*

EXPLOSION!

You do not want me to employ onomatopoeia for the sound that came out of Leo's diaper. It was deafening and surely woke the neighbors. I'm gonna save my editors some time and not even try to describe it because I know I'll get notes like "No one wants to read about your baby's poop" and "I hardly wanted to touch the page to turn it, there was so much poop all over the place."

So let's skip straight to the part where 25 minutes and one complete outfit change later (for Leo; thankfully he hadn't taken me down with him), we were ready to go. And now we really had to scramble in order to catch the next Air France bus.

We flew down the street, Mika making a racket with the luggage, me pushing the stroller as fast as I could without endangering our baby. We sidestepped landmines of dog poop, swerved around old ladies out for their morning stroll, and narrowly avoided tripping over the feet of the sleeping neighborhood drunk, before finally arriving right as the bus pulled up to the curb, sweat dripping from our foreheads.

Once safely on board, we tried to calm down. Stressing out wouldn't make the bus go any faster than its current snail's pace, thanks to construction traffic getting out of the city.

"Think we'll make it in time?"

"We've gotta try," Mika said, patting my leg.

Just then, Poop Machine decided we weren't stressed enough and threw up all over the place. I'm talking the scene from the Exorcist times two. That doesn't sound all that impressive but if I said times three or four, you wouldn't believe me. Times two… that's actually possible. And it happened. On my feet. And legs. On Mika's feet. And legs. And, worst of all, of course, on my poor baby Leo.

"Oh my God! I don't know whether to laugh or cry."

We cleaned up as best as we could, which is tough when you're wedged into a bus. We blew through our entire spare pack of baby wipes and I'm still not sure we got it all.

"Do you think he's sick?" I asked Mika. He'd had World War III in his diaper that morning but that was nothing new.

"Maybe he's just got motion sickness? He doesn't ride buses very often."

I hoped that was it, or this was going to be a long trip.

∽∾

When the bus arrived at the airport, we raced to the

terminal, still cutting it extremely close. I lost heart the minute I spotted the check-in line, but the lovely people at Air France insisted we jump to the front of the queue since we were traveling with a baby. They must not have smelled the puke from that far away otherwise I doubt they would have been so eager for us to approach their counter. Thanks to them, we made our flight with time to spare. Enough time for a pit stop in the bathroom to get Leo into a new set of flying clothes.

By the time we boarded, little man was hungry. I was still breastfeeding, which was a decision I had made a few months prior because I thought the trip would be easier if I didn't have to worry about heating bottles and washing bottles and carrying bottles. But now, as I settled into my narrow economy class seat, I realized I had a whole new set of troubles: bumping elbows and knocking elbows and generally having elbows all over the place.

I finally got Leo all set up and leaned back to try to relax.

"That's great you're breastfeeding," said the slightly older woman sitting next to me.

I smiled the International Airline Smile that means "I want to appear polite but I really hope you're not planning on talking to me the whole flight."

"How old is your son?"

"Four and a half months."

"Bravo. Women today give up breastfeeding way too soon."

I appreciated her congrats but it was still a bit judgy. What if I hadn't been able to breastfeed? Or what if I'd stopped? This total stranger would have been upset with my decision? I'd been back at work for a month at that point and I'd had to pump twice during the day in order to keep my supply up. Every time a colleague walked in on me (since I only had a semi-private place to pump) I questioned my decision and thought about quitting. But I'd wanted to at least try to make it to six months (because that's how long my mom breastfed me) and I'd wanted to "keep it easy" by breastfeeding during vacation.

Elbow to elbow with this woman, and my boob and son's head not much further away, I figured I should just let it go. The flight would be long enough without arguing over something my flight neighbor meant as a compliment. If we could just make it through the rest of the trip without another diaper blowout or a puking incident, I'd consider it a success.

≈

"OK, everyone. Line up!"

We were in Mom's living room getting ready for a family portrait. Mom and Doug, me and Leo, Stephen and his wife, Nikki, and my step-brothers, Justin and Eric. Jessie, Stephen's friend from high school who was now a freelance photographer, was figuring out how to best arrange us.

"Don't forget Mika," I said. "He should be down any minute."

He was upstairs in the bathroom, feeling pretty horrible. I knew it was a matter of seconds before he—

EXPLOSION!

—threw up all over the place.

From the sound of it, he might have made it to the toilet in time. But considering we could hear it all the way downstairs, I was worried what kind of state he and the bathroom were in.

Smoothing things over like a pro, Jessie continued. "He's really tall isn't he? Let's place him right here in the middle whenever he makes it down. OK, places everyone!"

After years of disastrous family photos, we'd decided to coordinate our outfits. That wouldn't fix Stephen's finger-stuck-in-light-socket hairstyle or the fact that Mom's eyes were always closed, but we had to control what we could. The boys wore white button-down shirts with black ties (even Leo!) and the girls wore solid-colored sweaters. Everyone wore jeans.

Mika stumbled down the stairs, his usually olive Mediterranean skin paler than a ghost. His shirt was unbuttoned and his tie hung loosely around his neck.

"You poor thing," I said, offering support without getting too close. "You look like death."

"That's exactly what I feel like. Are we ready? I was waiting until the last second to do my shirt up. I'm boiling."

"We're ready!" Jessie chirped. "I'll make it quick."

She snapped away at light speed, and then Mika changed out of his outfit faster than Clark Kent turns into Superman.

He headed back upstairs and treated us to Symphony No. 2, Puking in A Major.

Less than an hour later, I joined him.

ॐ☙

"Honey, wake up," Mika said.

"What time is it?" I asked.

"It's 3:00 in the morning. Leo woke up crying and is burning up. His temperature is 39.3 degrees."

Since we lived in France, and had therefore purchased our thermometer in France, we used Celsius. I didn't know off the top of my head what the Fahrenheit conversion was (but in case you're wondering, it's almost 103 degrees) but I knew it was really high. Like need-to-go-to-the-doctor-even-though-you-don't-have-American-health-insurance high.

Mika was finally starting to feel better, but I still felt rough. Coupled with having to breastfeed Leo every three hours, I hadn't gotten much sleep.

"I think we need to go to the ER, right?" Mika asked. "I'm not overreacting, am I?"

Of course this happened on a Sunday so even if we could find a pediatrician who would take a new patient on short notice, they wouldn't be open on a Sunday. Going to the ER would cost a fortune. But considering how bad Mika and I felt, and how contagious the bug was, we were sure Leo had the same thing. We had to take him. Correction, Mika had to take him. I could barely get out of bed and I was in desperate need of sleep.

I fed Leo while Mika woke my mom up and told her the fabulous news that not only did she get to wake up early, she got to drive them to the hospital. Ever the loving grandma, she jumped at the chance to help out. She didn't get to be a part of our daily routine back in Paris so she was thrilled to be able to lend a hand. I was thrilled to be getting a few hours of uninterrupted sleep. I just hoped Leo didn't have what we had, though I didn't see how he could have avoided it.

A few hours later, the trio returned from the ER with a clean bill of health.

"What? How is that even possible?" I asked. Not that I wanted my son to be sick, but there was no way he wasn't sick. Mika and I had been vomiting for the past 24 hours and Leo had been running a fever.

"They just said to give him medicine to reduce the fever and to keep an eye on his temperature," Mika said. "They sucked the snot out of his nose and put him in a little hospital gown. He actually thought it was awesome."

"I have a photo of him in his gown if you want to see," Mom chimed in, pulling her phone from her purse.

It was adorable. But still. "I'm scared to see the bill. They really just blew his nose and prescribed Tylenol? Sheesh."

As I predicted, minutes later Leo threw up everywhere.

And as I also predicted, the bill was astronomical. $1,400, to be exact. World's Most Expensive Tissue.

If we lived in the U.S., we would have had American health insurance and it wouldn't have been so pricey. Or, as we later realized, we could have gone to an urgent care center, which is much cheaper than the ER. But as people who were used to the French health care system, it had never occurred to us that we could be charged $1,400 for a quick emergency room visit, one that hadn't even required medicine or surgery. Had they given him a Prada hospital gown?

In the end, we were able to negotiate the bill to half-price by explaining we didn't have American health insurance and proving that our French health care didn't cover this situation. That was really cool of the hospital, but even at half-price it was still expensive. They could have at least given us this world famous tissue so we could frame it and show it to Leo later. "This is the tissue that cost us nearly one month's rent."

"Well, I know that was a pain," Mom said, "and I'm sorry you're all sick, but I'm so happy you made it to visit this year. I love you guys."

Lesson Learned #1: Always purchase travel health insurance when vacationing with children.

Lesson Learned #2: Always bring twice as many clothes as you think you'll need. They'll all get puked on, but at least you'll have something to wear while you're washing the first set.

Lesson Learned #3: No matter how much trouble it is, it's always worth visiting family for Christmas.

Tequila Tonic

If your stomach's upset, you're supposed to have crackers and tonic water. Boring! Then again, if your stomach's upset you shouldn't be drinking alcohol anyway. This recipe plays on the tummy-settling theme, while kicking it up several notches with a dose of tequila.

1 oz. tequila
2 oz. grapefruit juice
2 oz. tonic water
lime wedge

1. Fill a highball glass halfway with ice.
2. Add tequila, grapefruit juice, and tonic water.
3. Give it a few stirs, then squeeze in a wedge of lime.
4. Sip slowly to keep your equilibrium.

Makes 1 serving

22

Holiday Greenery

"Well, hello there," my dad said as he answered his phone. "This must be my lovely daughter. How are you? How are the kids? Still full of green boogers?"

It was Sunday afternoon Paris time, Sunday morning in sunny Florida. Dad fired off his signature three-question round of ammo, making me dizzy as I decided which question to respond to.

"We're all good, still full of green boogers." Bam! Replied to all three in one! "The kids are just getting over ear infections and now I have one myself."

"Oh, you poor thing. Does it hurt?"

Let's see... does it hurt. I felt intense pressure in my ears for a few weeks but let it slide because I was so busy with work and the kids and breathing oxygen that I didn't have time to wait in my always-two-hours-late doctor's office. Then one night I couldn't sleep because the pain was so intense—and remember this is coming from someone who birthed two children—until my eardrum finally popped. And proceeded to leak all over my pillow. I'm pretty sure leaking and popping aren't normal activities for a healthy ear. But I'd since been to the doctor and was now on the mend.

"It's getting better now that I'm on antibiotics," I managed to say, before coughing up nearly an entire lung. "Oh, and I've got a nice little bronchitis to go with it."

"So I guess you didn't mean it when you said you were all good?"

"Ha, no, I guess not. It's just that it's better than it was a few days ago so I feel I shouldn't complain."

"Well, keep your chin up and your nose clean."

People (namely, my booger-obsessed dad) had warned me that kids were germ machines, especially if they went to day care. They warned I would get sick. They warned I would spend all my time in doctors' offices. Somehow I hadn't believed them. But looking at my health insurance statements, I was about ready to ask for a punch card. "Buy 10 pediatric visits, get one free!"

A week later, the ear infection cleared up. The bronchitis passed. The kids had gone an entire seven days without getting sick. Things finally seemed like they were back to normal.

Then I dislocated my shoulder.

I was at work when it happened. It was kind of a little bit all my fault.

Let's back it up.

In January of that year, I'd gone into premature labor, though I wasn't due until May. I was hospitalized until the contractions subsided, but I remained dilated four centimeters (almost half the amount needed to give birth, for those of you who wanted more information in the cervix department) and was put on strict bed rest until the birth of my baby.

Fortunately (depending on how you look at it), I

remained on the couch for 14 weeks before giving birth. My baby girl came out fully cooked and completely healthy. Plus I got to skip work for 14 weeks. The only downside was my fat backside, which hadn't moved much in those last few months.

However, I had all summer to get rid of that as I chased my then two-year-old son around while hefting my newborn in her baby carrier. I had 16 weeks of maternity leave then took four weeks of vacation. Thank you France! Then, to polish it off, I took one month of unpaid leave until the day care center had completed their renovations (couldn't have done that over the summer, could ya?) and then I finally went back to work. On October 2nd. Have I thanked France yet?

While I enjoyed my time off, I now needed to get down to business. None of my tasks had been taken over in my absence (here's where I notably do *not* thank France) and I had loads to catch up on.

Except then the kids brought home green boogers from day care and infected my ears and lungs. So my first month back at work I wasn't operating on full steam. Though, I repeat, NOTHING had been done in my eight-month absence so even working at 50% of my usual hard-working pace was better than what my company had gotten used to.

Once my sickness passed, I hit the ground running. Literally. A customer reported a problem on our website and I met with every department in the building to try to resolve it. Finally, after talking to the head of our production facility downstairs, I raced upstairs to our open-air cubicle farm, armed with the answer to my problem.

In my haste, I missed a step on the stairs, grabbed the handrail to save myself, and that's when I dislocated my shoulder.

I blame myself because there was no reason to be

racing around. I was trying to prove that I hadn't gone soft while on maternity leave (though of course my thighs and midsection totally had). I was trying to prove that I was a hard worker even though I'd been gone for eight months (during which NO ONE did anything. Did I say that already? Because it REALLY needs to be said.) I was trying to prove that I was the same old kick-ass Vicki.

Instead, I got my ass kicked.

Part of it is due to my general clumsiness, a trait that my husband shares and a trait we've unfortunately passed on to our maladroit children.

Part of it is due to my post-pregnancy spaghetti ligaments that hadn't quite returned to their originally more rigid state.

And part of it is because of my eagerness to solve a problem.

So I'd really say that none of it was my fault, though you can hardly blame anyone else when you fall down the stairs if you were the only one there.

I didn't immediately realize I'd dislocated my shoulder. "Hrm, that hurt," I said, as a few Tweety birds floated by, followed by an entire solar system of stars. Yet that still didn't clue me in to the fact that something was wrong. I had a website to fix!

"Um, Vicki?" Camille, one of my co-workers, had a concerned look on her face. "Do you want to sit down a second?"

Did I want to sit down? No! I wanted to fix the... euh, wow. The room started to spin and I got really light-headed. I'd better sit down before I fainted.

She settled me into a rolling chair. "Let's have a look, yeah?"

I pulled the neckline of my shirt away to reveal my bone sticking out at a nauseating angle. I was really going to faint now.

"Coming through!" Another co-worker, Salima, charged through the gathering crowd. She leaned over me, her long brown hair falling in my lap, her perfectly lined red lips moving, but I didn't hear what she was saying. "Vicki! What day is it?"

"Um, *vendredi*," I managed. It was Friday.

"OK, that's good. Listen, I used to be a *pompier*. I need you to do what I say."

I nodded as I tried to get my head around the fact that our knockout accountant used to be a paramedic. *Les pompiers* were known for being attractive (they even put out a calendar each year) so that part was understandable. But I didn't get how you could go from saving lives to tracking invoices, especially in our boring office. The last time we'd had any excitement around the place was when someone set a bowl of candy next to the copy machine.

"Vicki? Are you listening?"

No. "*Oui*," I lied.

"OK, so Camille is going to call *les pompiers* and you are just going to sit here and eat this chocolate. It will keep you calm and keep your energy up. I'll go get you some pain medicine."

Chocolate? Good. Pain medicine? But I wasn't in any—OW, holy hell, mother-what-the-hell-was-that? I had just tried to reach for the chocolate and found out that dislocated shoulders are not only disgusting to look at, they're painful as hell. I also realized I'd been in shock up until that point. Black and white. Muted voices in a foreign language. Now I was living in vivid color with people shouting all around me.

Salima returned with a glass of water and two pills. "Here, take these," she said, tilting back my head and popping the pills in my mouth. "Let me lay this out for you. The paramedics will be here in a few minutes. They'll take you to the ER. You'll have to wait about an hour because even though it's probably the most painful thing you've ever experienced, you're not bleeding and you're not dying. So they'll make you wait while they take more urgent cases. Then they'll pop your shoulder back into place and send you home. You're looking at a couple, three hours."

I nodded, which in turn hurt my shoulder. I needed to remember not to do that.

"Don't do that," Salima said with a smile. "You're going to discover that way more parts of your body are connected to your shoulder than you thought."

She was right. Even chewing caused pain. I tried to focus on what I always focus on in times like these: What would I do if this were the zombie apocalypse? I would tough it out! I would pop my shoulder back into place! And I certainly wouldn't scream, wouldn't even whimper, lest a member of the living dead hear me and eat my brains.

Then I remembered a recent episode of *The Walking Dead*. A character had dislocated his shoulder and had left it that way for weeks—weeks!—until one of our heroes came along and helped him pop it back in place. They made it look so easy. And he had survived for nearly a month like that.

Which means TV is totally fake.

ᇰ∞ᇰ

The *pompiers* arrived, and what a team it was. A young woman who would have been pretty if she knew how to smile. A slightly chubby guy who didn't know he was slightly chubby and was still wearing his uniform from his less chubby days. And two other guys who were fine, just not exactly what you expect when a team of paramedics comes to your rescue. I doubted this bunch made it into this year's calendar.

Wow, I'm really shallow. That's no way to think about your knights and lady in shining armor.

"Get a load of this group," Salima whispered, jerking her thumb at the paramedics. "You get *pompiers* coming to your aid once in your life, and this is who you're stuck with? It's gone downhill since I left."

There, that made me feel better. And I realized it wasn't so much their looks, it was their attitude. None of them seemed happy to be there. I guess they were hoping for something more exciting than a dislocated shoulder.

That is, until they saw my shoulder.

"*Zut alors!*"

"*Oh là là!*"

"*Sacré bleu!*"

OK, they didn't actually say that because they aren't cartoon characters from the 50's. But the sentiment was the same: "Holy hell, that's bad."

Salima filled them in on the situation while I tried not to move.

"Ready?" the female paramedic asked. "Sébastien will escort you to the ambulance."

Wheee! I was gonna get to ride in an ambulance!

Sébastien helped me out of the chair, then steadied my arm as I inched past my nosy co-workers. I tried not to cry, but each step jolted my arm, despite having Sébastien for a human sling.

The paramedics helped me into the ambulance, where they suggested I sit in the seat instead of laying on the stretcher, reasoning it would hurt less. Yeah, but it wasn't as dramatic!

Then we drove over every speed bump in Paris on the way to the emergency room.

I tried to focus on the positive. I wasn't bleeding. I wasn't dying. The last time I was in an ambulance was when I thought my daughter was going to be born four months early. This was nothing.

BUMP!
But it still felt like something.

❧

"Breathe normally," the nurse said. "If you breathe too deeply, I'll take gas mask away."

I'd been admitted to the ER, examined by more people than had seemed necessary (I think some had just wanted to get a look at the Incredible Protruding Shoulder), had x-rays, and was now sitting topless on a stretcher, about to have my arm popped back into place. This prude American would have been embarrassed, but did I mention the gas?

"I will hold the mask over your face while they work on your shoulder," she said, indicating a stunning brunette doctor and a big, burly male nurse. They each gave a little wave.

"Sure," I mumbled.

"Where are you from, Madame?" the nurse asked. "I detect a little accent."

"St. Louis, Missouri," I whispered before closing my eyes and inhaling more gas.

"OK, you just think about St. Louis. You travel back to St. Louis, think happy thoughts, and breathe normally. If you take too much gas, I'll have to pull the mask away. We don't want you to faint. Nice and easy."

Nice and easy. St. Louis. Imo's thin crust pizza. Frozen custard. My mommy. OK, yeah, I think the gas was kicking in.

"Let's get started," the doctor said. "*Oh là là là là là là.*"

The excessive number of là's coming from the doctor got my heart racing, which increased my breathing rate.

"*Non, non, non,* Madame!" the nurse shouted, lifting my mask. "Tsk, tsk. I told you not to breathe too heavily.

We can't get greedy with the gas!"

I tried to slow my breathing. I was normally quite the rule-follower. I wasn't intentionally getting greedy with the gas, but if a doctor oh-là-là's you before a procedure, I think you're allowed to freak out.

"Go back to St. Louis..."

And I was back to la-la-land (the exact opposite of oh-là-là-land).

"OK, 1, 2, 3... POP!"

OMFG. OMFG. OMF—wait, that felt kind of good.

"*Ça va*, Madame?"

"Actually... yes. That feels much better."

It still hurt, and would for a few weeks, but they called me a cab and sent me off with some nice pain meds. Believe it or not, the worst part of my day was the car sickness from taking a taxi in stop-and-go traffic across Paris during rush hour.

ഐ

The best part, it turns out, was being off work for six days. Woo hoo! Party time!

Except for the fact that I'd only just returned to work after eight months off. And my arm was in a sling, so I couldn't do much. At least I didn't have to do any housework or change diapers, since my loving husband took care of that.

Then, just when I was ready to head back to the office, my bronchitis returned. I toughed it out and went to work anyway. How could I take more days off when I'd already been gone so long?

But after two weeks of nearly coughing my shoulder back out of its socket, I caved in and went to the doctor. It was the day of our office Christmas party. I planned to hop in to the doc, get a new prescription for genetically engineered super-strength mutant antibiotics, then head to the party.

My boss had been making an extra big deal about this year's party. I mean, yeah, who wouldn't get excited about drinking loads of free champagne and socializing instead of working?

But something was in the air. Something really big was going to happen at this party. I had to be there.

"*Voilà*," Doctor El Mouchnino said, signing an *arrêt de travail* with a flourish. "You're off work for the next three days. It's the only way to finally kick this bronchitis. That, and the new genetically engineered super-strength mutant antibiotics I prescribed you."

"But, but, I have a party to go to!"

His look said it all. No party.

"Also, you need to get a chest x-ray to be sure it's not pneumonia. Here's a prescription for that, too. *Bon rétablissement!*"

Get well soon? Not if I couldn't go to my party! I left Dr. El Mouchnino's office, head hung low, arm in a sling, coughing up both my lungs. You could practically hear the "wah, wah" of trombones in the background.

The next day I found out the big news from my co-workers: My boss was running for President of France. As in, the country. PRESIDENT. What a party that must have been.

And I had been lying in a pitiful heap on my couch, surrounded by green boogers.

Well, there's always next year.

Appletini

An apple a day keeps the doctor away, right? So to avoid green boogers, try this green apple cocktail. The logic is totally sound.

2 oz. vodka
2 oz. green apple liqueur
1 oz. apple juice

1. Add ingredients to a martini shaker filled with ice.
2. Shake, then strain into a martini glass, and enjoy the taste of not being sick.

Makes 1 serving

Family Matters

At the end of the day, the holidays are all about family

23

Auf Wiedersehen, Good Night

The plane touched down in St. Louis and I waited with impatience while people unloaded the overhead bins as if they weren't eager to see their significant other. Maybe they weren't.

I'd been in New York on a business trip and was supposed to return Thursday night but the client had requested I stay an extra day because I'm so awesome. Or, OK, because they realized I could help them with one more task, but if I hadn't been so awesome they wouldn't have realized that.

The New York-style pizza I'd had for lunch was now giving me heartburn as I tapped my foot in seat 24C. *Hurry up, fools,* I thought. I missed my boyfriend, Mark, and per our latest email exchange, planned to meet him at work before going out for a romantic dinner.

I grabbed a taxi and headed to his office, fortunately located not too far from the airport. I was so excited to see him I didn't even check my cell phone. You see, this was back when you had to pay roaming charges when you traveled to another state, back when Stegosauruses (Stegosauri?) roamed the earth. I'd had my phone with me in New York in case of an emergency and hadn't even turned it on since we landed.

We stopped in front of Mark's office and I flew out of the cab. I dashed through the lobby and down the hall (they really should get better security in that place), and spotted Mark fast at work behind the locked glass door of his lab. Finally I was here!

I rapped on the glass. "Mark!"

He looked up. "Oh, hi," he said. Then returned to whatever mad science he was currently working on.

That was it? I'd raced all the way from the airport for an "Oh, hi?" I motioned that I would wait in the side room but he didn't see me.

I settled into a swivel chair and figured now was as good a time as any to turn on my phone. I doubted I'd have any messages since Mark and I had been emailing all week and my friends knew I didn't turn my phone on when I was out of state.

My phone fired up and the ding of a new message surprised me. I had a missed call from my mom. I'd been emailing her all week, too. Nothing had been new. My grandpa was still in the hospital recovering from surgery but I'd visited him before I left and he had seemed OK. In rough shape, but he should totally get better. And Mom hadn't said anything in her emails about his health so I figured everything was fine. Maybe she just wanted to invite me to dinner? I wouldn't say no to a free dinner, but Mark would be pissed since we already had plans.

"Vicki, call me as soon as you get this." My mom's panicked voice filled my ears. "I didn't want to worry you on your business trip but I'm guessing you're home by now. Grandpa took a turn for the worse. He won't come out of it. Come to the hospital as soon as you can."

Shit. Shit shit shit. When had she left the message? How long did I have? I needed to go NOW.

I sprinted back to the lab, tears streaming down my face. "Mark! MARK! We have to go! Now!" I was beating the glass like a monkey at the zoo. Not very becoming but I didn't care. I had to get his attention.

He looked at me and held up his index finger, indicating for me to wait a second. The hell? Didn't he see the smeared mascara on my face and my primal fear? Get over here, asshole!

Finally, he strolled over and cracked open the door. "What's up?"

"Dude! What the hell? My grandpa is dying. We have to get to the hospital. Now."

"I need to finish my experiment. If I don't blah-blah-boring-science-thing before we leave for the weekend, then blah-blah-who-cares-it-doesn't-have-to-do-with-your-grandpa-so-blah-blah."

"You're going to make me wait and miss seeing my grandpa one last time?"

"Don't be so dramatic. I'm sure you have time. I can't ruin an experiment for this." He closed the door and returned to his petri dishes.

I called my mom while I paced the hallway, not knowing what else to do. "Hi Mom, I got your message. Why didn't you call me sooner?"

"Hi sweetie," she said, clearly shaken up, likely having just stopped crying herself a few minutes earlier. "I didn't want to worry you when I knew you were stuck in New York. But now that you're back, can you please hurry over? I don't know how much time we have."

"Yes, of course. I'm waiting for Mark to give me a ride. We'll be there soon."

The next twenty minutes felt like twenty hours. I hated his lab. I hated his experiment. I hated his calm coolness during a time like this. I thought maybe I even hated him.

"OK, ready?" he asked, as he appeared front of me, now changed out of his lab coat, car keys in hand.

I'd have to think about my feelings for him later. "I've *been* ready," I said, and turned to leave the building without so much as a hug or a kiss hello.

♥❧

"It doesn't look good," my mom said when we arrived at the hospital. "Grandpa formed several blood clots so they gave him some Heparin, but it turns out he's one of the few people who's allergic to it. His body is shutting down, one organ after another. There's no way he can recover."

I had a fleeting thought about how a hospital could get away with poisoning my grandpa, but realized it didn't matter. Screaming, suing, fighting, being pissed off wouldn't change the fact that my 72-year-old grandpa, the one who had cooked me "zoup" (his German way of pronouncing "soup") whenever I stayed home sick from school with him, the one who taught me that "Gesundheit" was the German way to say "bless you" after a sneeze, which he said numerous times during my sick days, was dying. And I'd almost missed out on a final goodbye because of Mark.

"I'll stay here all night. With you. With him," I said to Mom.

A few hours passed, and I found myself at least appreciating spending time with my extended family. It was a sad occasion, but a great opportunity to visit cousins and aunts and uncles I normally only saw during the holidays. With the exception of Stephen, who was deployed in Iraq and wouldn't be able to make it back, we were all there. We were prepared to stay as long as necessary.

However, a few hours had done Mark in. He was uncomfortable and hungry. Though I'd spent loads of time with his large yet close-knit family, he wasn't able to relax around mine. "Can we go? I'm starving," he said.

"There's a vending machine down the hall," I replied. "Or you can go and I'll get a ride with my mom later."

I stormed off to find my mom. "Can you believe him? What's his problem?"

"I know, honey," she said, wrapping her arm around my shoulder. "But maybe you should go. Try to have a normal night before you spend the entire day here tomorrow. Grandpa's stabilized. Why don't you grab dinner and meet us back here first thing tomorrow morning?"

I didn't want to leave. I'd already missed the vigil the past week. But I was exhausted from the business trip and was pretty hungry myself. "OK, I'll go. I'll be back first thing tomorrow morning."

I approached my sleeping grandpa in his hospital bed. I kissed him on the forehead. "I love you," I said, hoping against all hope that he could hear me.

❧

"I'll have the Caesar salad and a margarita on the rocks, extra salt," I said to our cheery waitress.

We were at the Cheesecake Factory, which had recently opened in St. Louis and only very recently had short enough lines to make it worth going. When they first opened, they'd hand you a buzzer and indicate a wait time of "up to two hours." And crazy fools would do it. Including us. Mark and I had gone once and saw a movie—an entire freaking movie—while we waited for our buzzer to go off.

Thankfully this night we'd only had to wait 15

minutes because if we waited any longer, we would have both died of hunger. My stomach dropped. How could I make jokes about death at a time like this?

I tried to enjoy the dinner. I tore off a few hunks of pumpernickel and sourdough from the bread basket, smearing them with butter and not caring about my low-carb, non-butter-smearing diet.

Mark seemed to be having a wonderful time. Well, why wouldn't he? It wasn't *his* grandpa on his deathbed.

I drank the last of my margarita and licked the salt off the rim. I don't know why I'd ordered such a festive drink at such a depressing time. It's not like a cheerful cocktail would change anything.

"What now?" Mark asked. "Do you want to go out downtown? Hang out at my place?"

"No. Can you just drop me at home, please? I want to get up early tomorrow."

He looked disappointed but I didn't care. I cried the whole way home. "I'll call you tomorrow," I said, getting out of the car.

"You want help with your luggage?" he asked, though he probably didn't mean it. No, that was being unfair. Of course he meant it. I was just upset.

"No, that's OK, I've got it."

I unpacked before heading to bed. I always unpack. Better to be prepared, even though all I wanted to do was cry myself to sleep. But don't worry, I did that too. Just after I unpacked and laid out my clothes for the next day.

⁓⁓

I woke the next morning in a great mood. It turns out, that was all a dream! You see, last night I had spent the night at Grandma and Grandpa's house, eating zoup and playing Skip-Bo. Grandma of course didn't let me win because she never let us grandkids win. "You'll never become a good player if I let you win all the time," she'd say. And she was right, though I suspect her policy was more due to her wanting to win than wanting to teach a lesson.

"Listen to your Grandma, Vicki," Grandpa said. "And then whoop her butt at Skip-Bo."

I climbed out of bed and saw my clothes laid out. What the...? Oh. Ohhhhhhh.

The truth hit me and I nearly fell to the floor. The dream had been that Grandpa was OK and that he wasn't dying. The reality was that I needed to go to the hospital for our final moments together.

Figuring I had a long day ahead of me, and totally kicking my diet out the window, I swung by the grocery store and picked up a case of donuts from the bakery. I'd get some coffee at the hospital. Even though the hospital's coffee was gross, I was too clumsy to allow myself coffee in my car. Always the practical one, I am.

I pulled into the hospital parking lot and took a deep breath. I carried the donuts in and headed straight to the Intensive Care Unit.

The nurse's station was empty, so I was able to walk right in to Grandpa's room. Except... no one was in there.

I had a sick feeling in my stomach, but maybe he'd just been transferred? Yeah, that was it! My dream *had* been true and Grandpa was doing better! They'd transferred him out of the ICU into a regular room. My family must all be there waiting for me. I had to hurry.

I returned to the nurse's station and looked around for anyone working.

"Hi, can I help you, honey?" a nurse said as she approached from behind.

"Hi!" I said brightly, turning around. "I think my grandpa got transferred. He was in that room over there but now I see it's empty. Could you please tell me what room he's in?"

Her face fell. "Oh, honey," she said, wrapping her arm around me.

She opened her mouth to say more but she didn't have to. I knew I'd gotten my hopes up for nothing. No one was here because there was no reason to be. He had died in the night and here I was, standing with my stupid donuts like an idiot.

"Thanks," I mumbled, then rushed out of there before the tears started to fall.

If this had been a movie, this is when I would throw the donuts in a trash can and storm out of there. Why do people do that? It's not the donuts' fault my grandpa died. There's no need to waste good food and fill a landfill just because someone passed away. Yet it felt wrong to walk out of the hospital with my frosted donuts, as if a sugar high would make us all feel better and forget that we'd just lost the patriarch of our family.

I trudged out to my car, in a daze, then slid the donuts on the passenger seat next to me. I decided to go to Mom's house. She had probably stayed up late with Grandpa and was trying to get what sleep she could before the day started.

When I arrived, I let myself in. Mom and Doug were sitting at the kitchen table.

"Oh, honey," my mom said when she saw me. She and Doug both rose and gave me a hug.

"I brought donuts," I squeaked.

And then I finally let the waterfall of tears tumble down.

❧

Six months later, my family arrived at Grandma's house for Christmas dinner. Half a year had passed. We were all mostly OK on a daily basis. Sometimes something would remind us of this great man (who, incidentally was The Smartest Man Alive and I know it's true because he told me) and the tears would come. But we were making it. You have to. Death is a normal part of life, and other stupid clichés that are supposed to make you feel better.

We felt he was too young to die, but we did at least get quite a few good years with him.

But now, gathered around the piano with the one off-key note, we all felt his absence. Profoundly. We sang out-of-tune Christmas songs. We ate cold food, because there's no other temperature when you're serving 55 people in one house. We chatted and tried to laugh and be merry.

Then it was time to open presents. The young kids tore open their gifts, as usual. The adults were more reserved exchanging their Secret Santa gifts (this was before Book Auction Mania took the family by storm).

Just when we thought we were done, someone spotted a huge trash bag behind the tree. How had we not noticed that before? Sure, it's easy for something to get lost amid the pandemonium of 55 people but you would have thought one of the curious kids would've scoped out the stash under the tree. Had the sack magically appeared?

One of my cousins dragged the bag into the center of the circle[4] and opened it to reveal 55 wrapped presents. Well, OK, it's not like we knew it was 55 right away, but as she handed one to each person, we saw that there were just enough for everyone.

In a coordinated effort, we all opened the gifts at the same time. They were beautiful Christmas-themed mugs,

---

[4] If you want to get technical, it was a pentacontakaipentagon, a 55-sided polygon. If you don't want to get technical, a circle will do just fine.

each one unique.

Who had done this? Who had left a bag full of gifts, one for each of us, under the tree without any of us seeing?

Grandma insisted it wasn't her. "When would I have had time for that? The church upped bingo to three times a week."

My uncles claimed innocence, my aunts feigned ignorance.

We all chose to believe Grandpa had come to visit us one last time, to give us one last gift, to share one last Christmas with us.

German Chocolate Cake Cocktail

My grandpa's German roots peeked through in little things he did. While he was more of a beer guy, I'm pretty sure I could have convinced him to try this decadent cocktail recipe as a tribute to his homeland.

3/4 oz. crème de cacao
3/4 oz. coconut rum
1/2 oz. hazelnut liqueur
1 oz. half-and-half

1. Add ingredients to martini shaker filled halfway with ice.
2. Shake, then strain into a martini glass (or your own unique Christmas mug), and enjoy the fact that it probably has fewer calories than a real slice of cake. But I'm not running the numbers, just in case.

Makes 1 serving

24

The Little Table

When 55 people gather for Christmas, there obviously isn't room for everyone at the official dining room table. Grandma and Grandpa always sat at The Big Table, the grandkids had to sit at The Little Table, and the other adults had to either fight for a spot at The Big Table or resign themselves to sitting on the couch or one of The Medium Tables set up in the basement.

"At least you get a table," my mom would say every year. "We always had to sit on the steps when we went to our grandma and grandpa's house." If I thought *I* had a lot of cousins, my mom had even more. And at every family event at her grandparents' house, situated on a farm in central Missouri, the kids would line up on the front porch steps and eat their meal on their laps. I doubted they did this in winter, but like the "We walked uphill to school in the snow both ways" line parents always spit out, you just nod and go along with it and let them enjoy their trip down memory lane, not even realizing you'll totally do the same thing with your kids one day.

Stephen loved sitting at The Little Table. "Mom doesn't nag me about my manners and I don't have to zip my pants up." Which isn't quite as pervy as it sounds because he was a kid and just wanted to stuff himself full of as much turkey and mashed potatoes as possible, and his only-worn-once-a-year-yet-still-always-too-small dress pants did not accommodate that plan.

One year, when he was five, his pants were so tight they literally burst at the seams, putting his Superman tighty whities on display. He didn't even notice it at first, so being the mean older sister I am, I let him run around—excuse me, fly around—in his superhero undies in the hopes of embarrassing him.

Finally, he asked why I was giggling. "Because we've all been staring at your butt for the past hour. You ripped your pants."

He looked down. "I don't see anything."

"I said your BUTT. Turn around."

He twisted around and saw his pants flapping around behind him. "I thought I felt a breeze! Oh well." He shrugged and ran off to play.

That is so not how I would have reacted. And that is so not how I expected my teasing to go! I was done with these little kids. I headed to The Big Table.

Grandma didn't reprimand me when I hopped up in the empty seat next to her, likely vacated by one of the smokers in the family. She continued talking and I tried to keep up.

"I don't know about this Dukakis character," Grandma said. "You think he'll win?"

"I sure hope not," one of my uncles said. "But I'm not so sure about Bush, either."

At school I'd heard kids calling the Democratic

presidential candidate "dookie caca," but I was pretty sure that type of dinner conversation wouldn't get me invited back to The Big Table. I kept looking for an "in" but at seven years old, precocious as I was, I couldn't convincingly debate politics.

Then they moved on to a topic I did know a little something about: babies.

I was one of the oldest cousins, so I got to play with each new little baby that came along. I loved holding them, rocking them, and giving them their bottles. What cute little story would my aunt tell about her new baby?

"This probably isn't for kids' ears, but..."

I looked around. I didn't see any kids. I gave her a look indicating the coast was clear.

Then she proceeded to talk about childbirth, which is ohmygod way different than talking about babies. I couldn't unstick myself from my seat. And I couldn't unhear that conversation. I tried to nod along, as if I totally understood what she was saying and wasn't totally terrified by it. Then, when she was done, I politely excused myself to go eat all the Christmas cookies and try to forget about things like "cervixes" and "epidurals" and "episiotomies," whatever the hell those were.

I set my plate of cookies down at The Little Table, a look of horror still on my face.

"Welcome back," Stephen said, grabbing a handful of cookies.

॰॰॰

These days I still sit at The Little Table, partly because my maturity level hasn't changed much since I was seven and partly because I now have two little ones of my own. Not that they do much sitting or even much eating for that matter. It's more dumping-contents-of-bowl-on-table and spreading-said-contents-all-over-the-place.

I had thought having French kids meant that by their very nature they would be well-behaved. I'd read all the books, I'd believed all the hype. Something in the Parisian air (apart from the pollution and smell of dog defecation) would ensure my little darlings sat at the dinner table for the entire length of the meal, took at least one bite of everything on their plates, and asked to be excused before going to ride their magic unicorns over rainbows. I was being totally realistic.

French kids don't throw food, right? Well, mine do. Maybe that's because they're half American and the not-throwing-food gene was overruled by the yes-let's-always-throw-food gene.

Or, come to think of it, it's probably my kids' parents who are messing it all up. Yeah, let's blame them! Burn them at the stake!

Wait a minute, that's me. And my husband. I take back that part about burning, though we can keep the part about blaming. It *is* probably our fault. Kids aren't inherently bad, are they? They're just inherent food-throwers who need parents to set limits for them.

In our defense, we are perpetually exhausted. We share a bedroom with both kids (hurray for tiny Parisian apartments!) and there are some nights where we get woken up every thirty minutes by one kid or the other, and sometimes we luck out with a double-whammy of both babies screaming at the same time. A sniffle here, a cough there, a tossing-and-turning like you've never seen. A toy falling with a thunderous thud, causing us to first think an intruder broke in, then play "Guess Which Toy Leo Snuck Into Bed When We Weren't Looking?" We're being held hostage by two cute dictators who are using sleep deprivation torture to weaken us into giving out information.

"Where's the candy, lady?" the two-year-old tyrant

asks.

"Candy!" the one-year-old chimes in.

"We'll give you anything you want, just let us sleep!" we both shout.

In my kids' defense, they are only one and two. I'm not sure all French toddlers sit nicely at the table and faithfully say *s'il vous plaît* and *merci*. I'd be willing to bet at least a few of them toss their *fromage* and *saucisses* on the floor, and cry over spilled *lait*.

We do teach them manners, and we try to be consistent. We set realistic rules, like "Use both hands when holding a glass" and "Don't throw applesauce at your sister." We don't even waste time on things like "You can't have ketchup for dinner" and "Don't use your shirt as a napkin."

Baby steps.

One day our children will (hopefully) be as well-behaved as their Gallic compatriots, but for now, if they can avoid picking their noses at the dinner table (we currently have a 42% success rate with that), I'm happy.

"*Maman*, some gouda would be gouda!" Leo says.

In the meantime, I'm glad they try different foods and repeat my lame jokes as if they're the funniest things in the world.

"But some cheddar would be better!" I say, getting huge laughs from an easy crowd. Yeah, I'm more than happy to be "stuck" at The Little Table with these guys.

Christmas Cookie Martini

This cocktail is for the adults, but takes its inspiration from the plate of cookies piled high at The Little Table.

1 oz. peppermint schnapps
1 oz. coffee liqueur
1 oz. Irish cream liqueur

1. Add ingredients to martini shaker filled with ice.
2. Shake, then strain into a martini glass. Optionally, serve with a plate of Christmas cookies, if the younger guests haven't devoured them already.

Makes 1 serving

25

The Most Wonderful Time of the Year

This year I'll celebrate my 35th Christmas. Thirty-five years of thinking, "Maybe this will be the year my family chews with their mouths closed and has calm, rational discussions." Ha, I don't think so.

But that's part of the charm. If everyone enjoyed a good Christmas meal and behaved themselves, we'd have nothing to talk about (or complain about or write books about).

By now it's seared into your brains that we'd have somewhere around 55 people at my grandparents' house. I repeat that number because it's amazing if you truly think about it. That number of hungry souls could fill a restaurant, easy. If you lined us up, we would span the length of a basketball court. Or you could stretch us for 2 ½ city blocks. But if you're done spanning and stretching us, could you please pass the gravy? We're trying to have Christmas dinner.

Our meal consisted of paper plates and cold food, constant chatter and glasses clinking. And at the center of it all were my grandparents. My grandfather's passing left a huge hole in my heart, and that first Christmas without him was tough. That didn't change, however, the raucous din 50-odd people managed to kick up. Conversations echoed off the hardwood floors and the show went on. After all, it was never Grandpa who had been making all the racket (except for a well-placed "dagnabbit" which I'm not sure is even a real swear word).

But now that Grandma has passed away, it's the end of an era. We feel both of their losses more acutely because we won't be celebrating at their house. We won't be celebrating with anyone of that generation. The next generation has taken over and scattered about. Smaller groups will have more intimate gatherings, where the headcount will reach a maximum of 10 people. We can count on real plates and warm food, even though we'd rather just have Grandma.

I wish Grandma would be coming to Christmas dinner this year.

I wish she would serve herself first ("I'm the oldest," she would explain) and ask me to fill her wine glass. I wish she would preside over the festivities with her ever-present smile. I wish she would talk with her mouth full (though I admit I won't miss her spitting green bean casserole particles on the side of my glass). I wish she would give me a Christmas card that says:

Merry Christmas!
Feel free to stop by anytime you like. Just call first.
Love, Grandma

I wish she would make us sing Christmas carols while one of the grandkids hammers on the piano, inevitably hitting the one out-of-tune key. I wish she would make us say grace when we really just want to dig in before our food gets even colder.

I wish she would be there to welcome anyone who didn't have any place else to go, and make them feel as if they were part of the family.

I wish, simply, that she would be there.

ღელ

I've always felt closest to my grandparents on my mom's side, but I've been fortunate to be blessed with six sets of grandparents. My dad's parents, my step-dad's parents, my step-mom's parents, and now my mother-in-law and father-in-law's parents. Wait, that sounds weird. My mother-in-law and father-in-law don't have the SAME parents. It's just that sentence was getting repetitive so I figured I should cut the "parents." Of course now I need this sentence to explain that sentence, so maybe I should have just left it in.

Anyway, six sets of grandparents, twelve delightful people, eleven of whom I had the honor of meeting, three of whom are still around to spoil me and pinch my cheeks.

My children have three sets of grandparents, six lucky souls who cherish their grandchildren, who drain their personal bank accounts to buy the kids gifts and who cook them "pancates" (Leo's still working on his English) and who pinch their cheeks.

From France to the U.S., we have family who loves us and fights (nicely) for our time over the holidays. It's not easy deciding where to spend Christmas (or getting time off work or getting cheap flights), but it's a good problem to have. So much family, so little time.

Who knows what future Christmases will bring? Laughter, joy, chaos, sadness. We'll likely be separated by an ocean from one side or the other, but we'll have memories of Christmas past, plenty of Christmas presents to be spoiled by, and will always look forward to future Christmases. Because it's the most wonderful time of the year.

The Night Cap

Happy Christmas to all, and to all a good night.
- Clement Clarke Moore, "A Visit from St. Nicholas"

1 1/2 oz. bourbon
1 1/2 oz. port wine
splash of orange liqueur

1. Fill a tumbler glass with ice.
2. Pour in all ingredients and stir.
3. Sip slowly, reflecting on the previous day, month, year. Then head to bed with sweet dreams of days, months, years to come.

Makes 1 serving

Acknowledgements

Thanks to Ellen Meyer, a.k.a. Mom, for encouraging me to write this book. I didn't know if I could do it, especially on the tight timeline we made for ourselves, but with your support I was able to bring these stories to life. I also didn't know if I could find 25 (interesting) tales about Christmas, but your impeccable memory saved the day. And thanks, as always, for editing and formatting my work and putting that extra coat of polish on it.

A big thanks to everyone else who edited and gave feedback on these pieces, including the people on the Métro reading it over my shoulder as I redlined during my commute. It really is a team effort!

Merci to Mika, who said, "You can do it!" even though I really wanted you to say, "Come sit on the couch while I rub your feet." Now that the book is done, though, I'll be cashing in on that offer of a foot rub. Big thanks to Leo and Stella, who do something new and cute every day, giving me writing material for life. I love you all infinity times infinity.

And, lastly, thanks to my liver. I haven't always been kind to you over the years, but you've stuck with me anyway.

About the Author

Vicki Lesage lives in Paris and writes about the ups and downs of her life abroad. Thankfully, there are more ups than downs, and at least the downs make for great stories!

Vicki hopes you enjoyed the book! If you did, she'd love it if you left a review at Amazon. For every review—even just a few sentences—Amazon sends Vicki a Christmas cookie. OK, not really. But Amazon does help convince other people to buy Vicki's book, which is arguably even better. Depending on the flavor of cookie.

Want more? Get *Confessions & Cocktails* for free! Simply join Vicki's mailing list: http://bit.ly/lesage-news.

Check out the other books in the Paris Confessions series:

Confessions of a Paris Party Girl, Vicki's wild Paris debut. Wine, romance, and a new life in France—a laugh-out-loud memoir from an American in Paris.

Confessions of a Paris Potty Trainer, the #1 Amazon Best Seller about Vicki's bumpy journey into motherhood and French parenting. If you think motherhood in America is a challenge, try navigating the City of Light with a stroller in one hand and a croissant in the other!

Petite Confessions, a quick glimpse into what Vicki's life in Paris is really like. You'll laugh, you'll cry, you'll want to open another bottle of wine.

Confessions & Cocktails, five funny stories paired with five fun cocktails for a quick taste of life in the City of Light.

Visit VickiLesage.com for more stories or drop Vicki a line at vicki@vickilesage.com.

Read on for a sneak peek of *Confessions of a Paris Party Girl*...

Get your groove on with...

Confessions & Cocktails

Drink up the good life in the City of Light!

If you've ever had one too many drinks and ended up spilling one too many secrets, this book is for you! This mini "memoirette" is a collection of stories about my life in Paris, designed to give you a taste of my writing style. Each vignette is paired with a sassy cocktail recipe that ties in to the theme of the essay.

So grab that cocktail shaker and let's get this party started!

Get it for free! Join Vicki's new release mailing list and she'll send you a free ecopy of *Confessions & Cocktails*: http://bit.ly/lesage-news.

Confessions
of a Paris
Party Girl

A HUMOROUS TRAVEL MEMOIR

1

Sister Mary Keyholder

I would like to say that when I first stepped off the plane and embarked on my new life in France, something memorable happened. Or something funny or amazing or romantic or at least worth writing about. Truth is, I don't remember. I take that to be a good thing. Considering all the mishaps I've had since moving here, "uneventful" nearly equals "good" in my book.

Looking back all these years later, I see myself as a hopeful, naive girl full of energy stepping off that plane. Tired of running into my ex-boyfriend seemingly everywhere around my midwestern American hometown, and having been unceremoniously freed from my IT job, this fearless 25-year-old was ready for a change.

I had dipped my toes in the proverbial European pond over the course of several college backpacking trips and now wanted to experience living there. To wake up to the smell of fresh croissants, to drink copious amounts of wine straight from the source, and maybe meet a tall, dark and handsome Frenchman. Who was, of course, not a wienie.

Oh, to be back in the shoes (or flip-flops, as it were) of that intrepid girl, arriving in a new land, successfully commandeering the Métro and her luggage, triumphantly arriving on the doorstep of her destination.

The smooth sailing didn't last long.

I had sublet an apartment for the summer from an unseen Irish girl, Colleen, using Craigslist. The photos showed a charming, yet tiny, apartment that I already pictured myself living in. You'd think this was where the story starts to go wrong, but the girl and the apartment did exist! Making it the last apartment to be legitimately rented online before scammers cornered the market.

For me, the issue was getting in to the apartment.

First I had to get the key. Colleen had agreed to leave it next door at the convent (Me? Living next to a convent? This'll be good.) The Catholic schoolgirl in me had an overly romanticized notion of how a Parisian convent would look. I was expecting some sort of Gothic cathedral with nunny looking nuns. So I must have walked past the modern, imposing structure about twenty times, sure I'd been conned, before I noticed the sign. Ahem.

I retrieved the key using a combination of my shaky French and the logic that, c'mon ladies, how would anyone else have found out about this bizarre scenario and come knocking on your door?

"Bonjour, je m'appelle Vicki. Comment allez-vous?" I asked the group of navy-blue-clad, pious-looking women gathered inside the doorway.

The elderly (aren't they all?) nun closest to me cautiously replied, *"Pas mal. Et vous?"*

Ack! What did she say? I was so busy forming my question I didn't plan for her response! Just keep going, you can do it. *"Je cherche une clef."* I'm looking for a key.

"*Une clef?*"

"*Oui, une clef.*" Now I know that's not much to go on, but let's be real. Do lost girls often come to their door? Hrm. Now that I think about it, maybe that's how girls become nuns? Better speed this up before I get stuck in the nunnery, never to be seen again. "Colleen leave key? It's for me."

"Oh yes, a key! For an American girl. That must be you." Was it that obvious? Was it my blonde hair? Wide, toothy smile? No, it was probably my command (or lack thereof) of the French language.

"You're friends with Colleen?" she asked.

I wasn't sure how to answer that since we weren't really friends, but then again I wasn't even sure that was the question. My French wasn't up to the task of explaining how I knew Colleen, and for sure if I said we weren't friends, Sister Mary Keyholder would never hand over the precious key.

"Yes," I said with a smile, then promptly got the heck out of there.

Key and two heavy suitcases in hand, I headed to my new apartment building. The number on the front, 20, was written in the ornate curlicue script that most French buildings employ. The large windows of each apartment were fronted by black wrought-iron rails, providing the perfect vantage point from which to observe the goings-on of the street below. I eagerly punched the five-digit code into the digicode reader to the right of the door and was in.

Next issue: finding the actual apartment. You'd think this would be easy since Colleen had said it was on the third floor. Silly me, that seemed like enough information until I scoped out the situation.

Problem 1: Once inside the front door, I saw two buildings – one that faced the sidewalk (in which I was currently standing) and one past a quiet courtyard containing a few trees and a large, overflowing trash barrel. Which building was it?

Problem 2: Colleen had said the apartment was on the third floor but in France the ground floor is counted as the "0th" floor, so what an American calls the third floor, a French person calls the second floor. I didn't know if Colleen had adjusted for the American way or stuck to the French method or if Ireland had an entirely different technique[5].

Problem 3: Each floor had two apartments.

So I had a total of eight possible apartments to choose from, none of which had names on the door. I was afraid to leave my bags unattended so I schlepped up the first set of stairs, bags and all, and knocked on each door. On any door where I didn't get a response, I tried my key. No dice in any of the apartments in the first building, so I hauled my luggage down the stairs and through the courtyard to the second building. One person answered and had no idea who Colleen was (friendly neighbors!) and I tried my key in the other three doors. But again, no dice. Crap! After trying eight

---

[5] I've dedicated many a conversation to this topic because that's the kind of life I lead (if you understand that, you're going to *love* this book) and I still can't tell which system is better. I can see counting the ground floor as the first floor because it has a floor and it's the first one you walk on. But I can also see the logic in going up your first flight of stairs and then counting "1", then another flight and saying "2" and so on. I mean, are you trying to get credit for making it to the ground floor when you haven't even gone anywhere? When you're not in a building do you say you're on the first floor? No, because you're just on the ground! So I guess we'll have to call it a wash. Sit back and relax – I'll take care of sending the memo to America and France so they know what I've decided on this important matter. And I still don't know how they do it in Ireland!

different apartments, one of them should have been the right one.

I sulked down to the courtyard and let out a few choice words of frustration. I thought back to when my mom and step-dad, Doug, were seeing me off at the airport. We had a tearful goodbye and I choked up when my mom said "Good luck in your new life, honey." She was sad to see me go but wanted me to be happy. And now here I was, trapped outside my new apartment, admittedly not doing so hot in this new life.

I wanted to call her and cry but I needed to get into the apartment to get the damn phone! Plus, I didn't want to give Mom a heart attack by waking her at 5:00 in the morning. No, better to sort everything out myself and call when I had good news to report.

I straightened up and reassessed the situation. I know I'm at the right address since the front door code worked. Colleen hadn't said anything about crossing the courtyard, so her apartment is probably in the first building. And since we're in France, she had probably used the French system of floor numbering.

Not giving a rat's ass about the suitcases anymore, and hating their guts for being so stubbornly heavy, I hauled my sweaty self up the first stairs once again and tried both apartments on the (French) third floor.

Funny thing, no matter how determined you are, if the key ain't right for the door, it ain't gonna open. And this key was a monster. At least twice as large as a standard door key, it squirmed of its own volition, so determined was it to not fit in the door.

Now I was dejected. I went back to the sunny courtyard to throw insults at my luggage and half-seriously glanced around for a place to sleep. Behind the trash bin? Under the tree? Maybe with enough vin rouge I could make the courtyard comfortable. I turned to the sky for answers (why do people do that?) and that's when

I noticed the burgundy curtains in an apartment on the third floor of the second building. I recognized the color from one of the Craigslist ad photos. At last! This could be it. So looking at the sky does provide answers.

Leaving the luggage once again, I climbed the stairs and tried the key in the door. It wasn't easy going, but I was more determined than ever. I shimmied and I shook. This key had to fit! I was NOT sleeping under a tree!

With vigorous jiggling, cursing, and promising my firstborn child, the door finally opened. I'd never been more proud of myself in my life. I might have even literally leapt for joy. "Hello, Paris! Vicki is here and watch out, she can OPEN DOORS!"

After touring my new digs, I mustered up the strength to retrieve my luggage. Me! And my bags! In my apartment! With a key that opens doors! Wheee! The possibilities in this new life are endless. If I can open a door, I can do anything!

Find out what happens next... buy *Confessions of a Paris Party Girl* today!

CATCH UP ON THE
Confessions Series
BY BESTSELLING AUTHOR VICKI LESAGE

For deals, news releases, and a free ecopy of
Confessions & Cocktails, sign up here:
http://bit.ly/lesage-news